One Student at a Time

A Teacher's Journey

I hope you enjoy my journey!

Ken Rand

KEN RAND

Fulton Books, Inc.
Meadville, PA

Published by Fulton Books 2020

ISBN 978-1-64952-021-0 (paperback)
ISBN 978-1-64952-023-4 (hardcover)
ISBN 978-1-64952-022-7 (digital)

Printed in the United States of America

Reviews and Endorsements

WOW!! I love the chapter about "Dr. Davis" and the stories about all of your students. It feels like I'm reading a memoir from a gifted teacher who also happens to be a gifted storyteller. It's my second read, I still cried and laughed even though I already knew what was about to happen. I hope someone makes a movie out of it. I know this is a diamond! I can't wait to see it on the bestseller list everywhere. Every teacher I know is getting this book for Christmas or if it is printed later, I will buy copies for Teacher Appreciation Day! Ken, BRAVO, and Congratulations.

P. Garcia

You're right. I should've heeded your advice in having a box of Kleenex nearby. I can't say I liked it because like doesn't cut it. I was moved because your stories were fully loaded with such power but delivered with simplicity and a very humble, sincere tone which any person can relate to, teacher or not What can I say, I immediately felt a rush of emotions while reading your book. I hope someone is smart enough to make it into a movie. At some point in time, probably every single person who worked a new job had all those same emotions you did so I could relate immediately.

V. Keller

This book is GREAT and is a wonderful read. I've thoroughly enjoyed the book and laughing out loud (where appropriate).! I can picture it as a movie. Ken Rand tells his story in a way that makes me feel like I have both a mentor and a best friend. I highly recommend this book for everyone—whether you are also a teacher, like myself, or you can recall ever being inspired by one. It's laugh out loud funny in a Mrs. Maisel sort of way, but Rand's depiction of his growth over this long career and how he learns to make meaningful connections to his students is both timeless and applicable to anyone wanting to make a difference in the world.

H. Yelland

Your book, is incredibly great! Witty, warm, and wise, as reviewers used to say. The stories of Jacque and Michael and Dorothy and Patricia are really moving and captivating. And it was great to read about your dad playing piano for your students, and with Dirk Etienne as well.

J Riley

Books by Ken Rand:
- Time Cards and Paychecks, Janus Publishers
- Beginning Algebra: Solving the Mystery, Ken Rand Publishing
- Handy Math: Focus on Sports (w/Jan Fair), Creative Publications
- Handy Math: Focus on Travel (w/Jan Fair), Creative Publications
- Handy Math: Focus on Purchasing (w/Jan Fair) Creative Publications
- Point-CounterPoint (graphing activity book), Creative Publications
- Habits of the Mind (contributing author), Stylus Publications
- Afterwords (word game book), Ken Rand Publishing

Games by Ken Rand:
- Dominque: Great Games
- Dotto: Tega-Rand
- Shanghi Rummy: Brio International
- In the Chips New York: Tega-Rand
- In the Chips Hawaii: Tega-Rand
- Runners World Marathon: Tega-Rand
- Closure: Ken Rand Publishing
- Random (word games): Ken Rand Publishing

Contents

It's 1968. I am in my first year of teaching at a JHS in the Southeast Bronx. I am 21 years old. Martin Luther King is assassinated and Michael, a black student who is a major behavior problem, finds a way to validate who I hope to be as a person.

For a totally lost graduating college senior, becoming a teacher in an inner-city junior high school in New York was a completely unplanned and unexpected destiny.

My poor study habits and quick thinking, lead to a surprise outcome in my freshman economics course in college.

My brother and I were once professional dancers. His competitiveness on a TV dance contest has an undesirable result (for him).

My dad goes ballistic when he finds out that I signed up for the Peace Corps upon graduating college. Uncle Meyer's call to me the next day totally changes the direction of my life

My students love me. One major problem. I didn't know how to teach. When too many of my algebra students failed the NY State Regents Final Exam, I wanted to quit teaching. That failure became a turning point in my career. I would never allow this to happen again.

There are some great "teacher" movies that I have used in my classroom to help inspire my students. Using videos that have nothing to do with math helps me teach my students about life and about learning. "Your best is not good enough" is a quote from one of those movie videos that opens their minds to new possibilities.

In order to fully understand how Michael's classmates are able to change his life, I need to introduce you to "The Program". The premise of The Program is positive peer pressure and it worked.

I now have 19 of the worst behaving students in my special Program class. How do I convince them that this innovative approach to discipline problems will work? Read and you will find out.

My dad's talents as a musician help make me a hero with my Program students but it also prompts another visit by me to the principal's office. Is this the time I get fired?

The students in The Program perform their magic and I get to witness a classroom miracle on Michael. If I was not there to witness it, I would not believe it. Hope you kept the tissues close by.

Not all teaching problems occurred in the classroom. Enough said.

My interview for my first full-time community college teaching position is one for the books. Questions attacking my credibility make for an interesting hour. My community college teaching future depends on how I handle this inquisition.

The college president, at the first faculty meeting of the year, over does it when he introduces me to the entire faculty. In doing so, he unintentionally puts a target on my back that takes me years to remove.

In my first year at Hartnell Community College, I get called down to the Presidents Office. Not knowing what to expect, I am introduced to a student (Dirk) who has a fear of mathematics. After 30 years, Dirk and I are still friends.

In 2009 the math and science departments at the college are the recipients of a $3 million dollar grant. That summer, using some of these funds I create the Math Academy which becomes the most successful grant program in the college.

A college supervisor tries to take control of the Math Academy, my resistance causes a personality conflict which leads to my published Algebra textbook to be banned from the college bookstore. Another windmill to defeat

After failing algebra four times with four different teachers, I am Patricia Garcia's last hope to fulfill her dreams of passing math and graduating from community college. Her refusal to give up and her remarkable road to success is one of the reasons that I became a teacher.

I wake up one morning and realize that it's time to retire. But am I truly finished yet? Hmmm?

Author's Note & Acknowledgements

I consider myself to be a very lucky man. I remained in one profession that I love for forty-seven years. Going to work each day was not really going to work. Teaching was never a job to me. It was a passion. Each day was a learning experience that was filled with its ups and downs (mostly ups) that helped to define who I am as a person.

This book has a long history. I actually started to write it way back in 1975. At that time, I wanted to document some of the incredible experiences I had while teaching in a New York City Junior High School, especially those pertaining to "The Program." My original title for the book was "The Successful Failure," and after reading my current book I think you will understand my reasoning for that choice.

However, as they say, life seemed to get in the way and those original seven hand typed chapters (computers were not yet invented) remained stored in a box in my garage for the next forty years.

When I retired from teaching in January of 2015. I realized that I had a lot more stories to tell but I had a dilemma. I wanted to both share my amazing stories and simultaneously have part of the book used as a guide for those "how to teach" chapters. Shortly after retirement my sister-in-law Linda Rand told me that the book, "Teacher Man" by Frank McCourt was a "must" read and she also relayed how his teaching experiences reminded her of my own. She even strongly suggested that I write my own novel.

And that's exactly what I did. Part One of my book was devoted to sharing those fascinating stories and Part Two was reserved for the "teaching" concepts. However, there was one major problem. When I sent my book to a number of publisher's, I continually received this repetitive feedback. "Your stories are compelling and captivating, but we don't think there is a market for this type of format."

What to do?

In October of 2019 I read a book written by my cousin Dr. Ken Harris. His book, "Synchronicity: The Magic, The Mystery, The Meaning (a current best seller) is a collection of stories that Ken has experienced that go beyond the concepts of chance or coincidence. It was immediately after reading his book that I realized that I may be able to capture a much broader audience if I simply wrote about all of the amazing experiences that I have had in my forty seven year journey as a teacher. Perhaps, at some later time, I may be able to publish my thoughts on "How to teach" as a separate book. I then immediately set out on the task to reorganize my book as a complete collection of these amazing stories so that it would read as a memoir.

I hope you enjoy these stories and allow yourself to experience this journey through my eyes.

I want to offer a special thank you to my first editor Karen Cheatham for her role in making me a better writer. My son Kevin, who is also an editor, was very influential to me and constantly let me know that my best was not good enough as he inspired me to rewrite and rewrite and rewrite some more until I my words had a greater meaning and clarity.

Thank you to all of my friends, relatives and colleagues, especially Patricia Garcia and Linda Sachs Rand, who took the time to pre-read my manuscript and whose suggestions and critiques helped me to make vast improvements in the organization of my book. I would also like to thank Jennifer Fletcher for her early guidance and encouragement for me to pursue my dream to complete and publish my memoirs.

It would also be impossible for me to have written this book without the influence of all my students who found, on a daily basis, a way to challenge me and make me a better teacher. There are just way too many of you to thank by name.

Most importantly, I would like to thank my family for their support and love.

Some of my stories took place long time ago (40 – 50 years) and the passage of time can wreak havoc on one's memory. With that in mind, I want to thank my cousin Ken and my sister-in-law Linda for helping me recall specific names, and dates. I have purposely restrained myself from embellishing my recounts of these amazing experiences in order keep the stories authentic. What you are about to read is exactly what happened.

Put on your seatbelts and enjoy the ride.

Chapter One
Michael

Since I am a teacher, I'll begin with a no-stress, extra-credit question for you:

Who said the following:

"There are two kinds of teachers: The kind that fill you with so much quail shot, that you can't move, and the kind that gives you a little prod behind and you jump to the skies."

    a)   Jaime Escalante
    b)   Albert Einstein
    c)   Ken Rand (me)
    d)   Robert Frost

The answer is at the end of this chapter.

Michael (Story No. 1)

Michael Hadley was a thirteen-year-old teenager who was transferred into both my seventh-grade homeroom class and my general math class. This transfer happened during the latter part of my first year of teaching—1967/68—at a junior high school in the Bronx, New York. Exactly how and why I became a teacher is a great story and the subject for another chapter.

In 1967, the very unpopular Vietnam War was in full gear. Those of us who grew up in this era can remember how newspapers, on their front page, would keep a daily total of Americans killed in action. I can still remember the sick and uneasy feeling of seeing this number increase every day. American boys not trained to fight in jungles are doing exactly that.

Teachers, fortunately for me, are temporarily exempt from the military draft and able to avoid the war. This is not the reason I became a teacher, but it was a factor leading to that decision.

In 1967, heavyweight champion Muhammed Ali was convicted of refusing to be drafted into the army. Four years later, in 1971, the Supreme Court overturned that conviction. Not having committed a crime, he lost four years of his professional career.

The year 1967 was also a time when there was civil discord, unrest, and organized marches and riots throughout the country. TV news had appalling images of peacefully protesting blacks being painfully hosed down by police with fire hoses. Lyndon Johnson was the president, and Martin Luther King was heading the civil rights movement. Our country was clearly going through a difficult time. But it was also a time when those of us under the age of thirty are becoming politically and morally involved in the future of our country.

Music was also a big part of our lives. The Beatles, who arrived on the American music scene in 1963, were still on top of the record charts with their album *Sgt. Pepper's Lonely Hearts Club Band*. Among other big recording hits were Aretha Franklin's "Respect" and "Light my Fire" by Jim Morrison and the Doors.

In 1967, you could go see a double matinee movie (with twenty cartoons) for just 95 cents. This is the year that the movie *The Graduate*, starring Dustin Hoffman, was nominated for "Movie of the Year." The song from that movie, "Mrs. Robinson," by Simon and Garfunkel, was a number one hit for over ten weeks. Postage stamps are only 5 cents and gasoline costs 33 cents/gallon. As I am writing this, there's a voice in my head that is now singing "Those were the days, my friend…"

It was an amazing time in history. It was a great time to be twenty-one and naive. But not such a great time to be a teacher, especially a teacher with absolutely no experience teaching in an inner-city school.

My seventh-grade homeroom classroom was a typical New York City junior high school classroom. It was average in size, about 20 feet by 30. The desks and chairs were old and worn out. There wasn't a single desk in my room that didn't have some profound words of wisdom carved into it, such as "This teacher sucks" or "I hate school" or "Duke sat here." *Duke, no one cares that you sat there. Who names their son Duke, anyway?"*

It took me about a month to realize that these meaningless desk carvings were just warm-up and practice for what was written on the boy's bathroom walls. The stalls in the boy's bathroom had writings and graphics on them that defy the English language. I don't feel comfortable repeating them here, you can use your imagination.

The blackboard in my classroom was older than me with inconvenient cracks in it. It would be another twenty years before the city would get progressive and change them to greenboards. The classroom ceilings were really high, about 18 feet. I could never understand why they were so high. *Do students grow that much in junior high school?*

Erasers and chalk were a rare commodity. Somewhere in the school, there was an eraser thief. I often fantasized about putting up posters all around the school saying: "Wanted Dead or Alive! Reward: $100 or a free supply of erasers for a year for anyone catching the Eraser Thief."

Funny thing is that, out of necessity, I would soon join the infamous club, the EBAC (the "Eraser Bandits Anonymous Club"). I became so good at stealing erasers that I nominated myself to be president of the EBAC. I even developed a great scheme to covet the priceless eraser. I would (illegally?) dismiss my classes one to two minutes early then run through the halls to my next class. If there was no eraser in it (which had a high probability), I would have just enough time to search the rooms nearby for that elusive eraser. Smart, huh?

It took me a couple of years to realize that it would be even smarter to carry my eraser with me throughout the day. One major problem, chalk dust. It's just not cool to have chalk dust all over my freshly dry-cleaned suit.

My classroom, like most of the rooms in the school, had large windows facing a street. The nearby neighborhood scenery of small private homes was pleasant and just pleasant enough for students to look out and daydream thoughts of not being in school. The wall opposite the windows had collapsing doors that hid clothes closets for students. Not that they would ever use it. No experienced student trusted their coats would be there at the end of the day.

Don't get me started on the teacher lounge. I think I'll save this for another chapter. Back to Michael.

Michael was a slender and lanky African American young man, weighing around 120 pounds and standing about 5'8". That's pretty tall for a seventh grader. He had a beautiful, black complexion, pearly white teeth, and big, bright eyes.

Shortly after Michael was transferred to my classes, I found out that I was the fourth teacher to have Michael as a transfer student. He was the sixth male student to be transferred to my classes in a six-week period. I was beginning to see a pattern. Michael, like so many of the other transfer students, came into my class because he was having behavior problems with other students and teachers. I only had a few seats available when Michael was transferred to my class, so he sat in the last row in the back of the room. I'm thinking, *The further the better.* Any teacher reading this is now saying "Yep."

I also remember wondering, *Why me? Was I being punished or rewarded? Give me a break. I am still in my rookie year as a teacher, I'm only twenty-one years old, I'm a kid teaching kids. Why does Freyer keep sending me these students?*

For some reason, unknown to me, Dr. Freyer, the school principal, has decided to send the most challenging kids in the school to a young, very young, and naive me. Thinking on the positive side, perhaps Freyer—everyone called him Freyer—could see I had a knack for building a rapport with even the worst of students. One major problem: I don't know how to teach. My principal knows it, the other teachers know it, I know it, and worst of all, my students know it.

Unlike the other students who were part of the weekly parade to my classes, Michael wasn't a tough guy. Most of the students transferred to my classes had reputations for starting—and ending—fights with classmates and teachers. Michael, on the other hand, had a different kind of problem and reputation. Michael was constantly moving in his seat, and it was a rare occasion when he was in his seat at all. There were many times (too many) when he would spontaneously get out of his chair, randomly walk around the room, and begin a conversation with anyone who would listen. He would also love to talk to anyone who happened to be sitting next to him. Plus, he had an uncontrollable habit of talking out in class.

Though Michael was on the safe side of crazy, he was harmless and was not a physical threat. But there were times, however, when he made it almost impossible to teach. You can imagine, or maybe you can't, that he was extremely annoying to his classmates. His misbehavior was even more annoying to me. Michael was the epitome of the type of student that gave teachers nightmares. If Michael were evaluated today, my guess is he might be diagnosed with ADHD.

My education professors in graduate school never bothered to teach me how to handle a student like Michael. In fact, they didn't teach me how to handle any student. Looking back at my graduate classes over the summer of '67, I was not taught a single thing about how to create a rapport with students. The truth is that I really didn't learn anything at all about "how" to teach while in graduate school. Nada, nothing, zilch. In the late '60s, there was a shortage of teachers, especially in the inner-city schools, and we were rushed through a two-month program for the main purpose of filling that void.

For me, creating a rapport with my students was merely a matter of survival, and in this regard, my young age was, perhaps, an advantage. The one contradictory and repetitive piece of advice that I did receive from my veteran colleagues was "Don't smile for the first two months." However, you don't have to be a genius to figure out that it's not easy building a rapport when you don't smile. I ignored that advice because it just wasn't who I was. I'm twenty-one years old. I smile all the time.

I was also warned not to show any anger toward my students. "Never, ever, get into a shouting match with a student. They will eat you alive." This was great advice, and my students found a way to test me every single day.

Over a short period of time, Michael and I began to build a connection with each other. He would still, however, manage to find ways to be disruptive. I can remember, the many (too many) days after trying to discipline him, when the thought of pulling out some of my bushy and curly hair was occupying my brain while I drove home from work. Again, while I am driving, I am also shouting in my head, *Why me? Why me?* It was difficult enough trying to find ways to transfer my math knowledge to my students, now I had to also be a counselor, a policeman, a parent, an entertainer, and a psychologist.

Little did I know that on one fateful morning, Michael would teach me more than I could have ever learned from any colleague or from any graduate-school classroom.

The date was April 5, 1968. It was the day after Martin Luther King was assassinated. I was with my seventh-grade homeroom class. Michael had been in my class for about two months.

Early that Friday morning, while we were still in our homeroom class, there was an announcement over the school loudspeaker. The assistant principal said that we would soon have a moment of silence in honor of Dr. King. I clearly remember that I was sitting at my desk in front of the room during the announcement. My head was down on my desk, trying to hold back my tears and emotions for the loss of the man I so admired. I was saddened by the death of this great man and also feeling ashamed for being white. A white man, James Earl Ray, had killed Dr. King, and for some reason, I just felt the guilt of a nation.

During this moment of silence, as I was sitting at my desk with my head still down, I could hear many of my students crying. It wasn't long before there wasn't a dry eye in the classroom. All my students—black, white, or Hispanic, it didn't matter—were all shaken by the tragedy. (In my seventh-grade homeroom class, about half of my students were black, about 40 percent were Puerto Rican, and the rest were white.)

During our grieving, while I was trying to focus on our collective pain, I heard a chair moving in the back of the room. I momentarily picked up my head and saw Michael get out of his seat as he to often did and I remember thinking, *I just wasn't in the mood to deal with him. Not now, Michael.*

I ignored him and immediately put my head back down, holding it in my hands with my elbows on the desk. Except for the sound of crying, there was a cold silence in the room. Through that silence, I could hear Michael's footsteps as he slowly walked up to my desk. Without hesitating, Michael came right up to my desk, looked at me, and said, "What's wrong, Mr. Rand?"

Now I'm thinking, *Huh? What? This is not the disruptive Michael that I know.* I could plainly sense the compassion and empathy in his voice. I told him, without looking at him, "Michael, there are no words to express to you how I feel right now."

And then Michael—crazy, uncontrollable Michael—surprisingly put his arm around my shoulder to comfort me. *What's he doing?* He then said with a slight smile, "Don't worry, Mr. Rand, I understand. I know how you feel. You and me, we are the same color."

This was a *wow* moment for me. A black national hero just got assassinated by a white man, and this black student, a too-often misbehaving black student, tells me, a white teacher, that he and I are the same color. To this day, what Michael said to me has been one of the most beautiful and meaningful things ever said to me in my entire life. In doing so, he validated who I hoped to be as a person. If you take a minute to absorb what Michael said to me, you, too, will understand the beauty of his thoughts.

In three short months after Dr. King's assassination, on June 5, Democratic candidate and front runner Robert F. Kennedy was assassinated as he was leaving a campaign rally in Los Angeles. Two weeks later on June 19th, there was a march on Washington, DC, sponsored by the Poor People's Campaign.

I had to go.

I soon found out that some of the black teachers in my school were planning on taking the bus ride to Washington and decided to go with them. To my dismay, I was saddened by the fact that I was the only white teacher on a bus full of fifty people. During that two-hour trip, I think I learned every freedom song ever written. I just wish I could sing.

After the eventful march, we arrived, by bus, back in Manhattan about 12:30 AM. We tried to get a taxi to stop for us, but no luck. My colleagues told me that they would stand away from the street so that it would be easier for me to flag down a cab. Within one minute, a taxi stopped for me, and my three colleagues ran out and got into the cab with me. In spite of the blatant racism exhibited by taxi drivers, we laughed all the way back to the Bronx.

The late sixties was definitely a time of social injustice and social conscience. The nation was divided, but for the first time, more and more people were beginning to become part of the movement towards racial equality. It's now over fifty years later, and this is beginning to sound all too familiar.

I have absolutely no tolerance for racial injustice. People today say that we need to listen to both sides. I'm sorry. There is no other valid argument for the other side. My mom taught me right from wrong.

Michael obviously had a golden heart, and the goodness in his heart kept him from looking at me as a white teacher. My eyes still swell up when I tell this story during my public speaking.

God bless you, Michael.

There's more. Get ready for some other *wow* moments. There is another great story about Michael (chapter 16) when Michael becomes the recipient of a classroom miracle, but first I would like to tell you how and why I became a teacher.

The answer to the extra-credit question is Robert Frost.

Chapter Two
Let's Start at the Beginning

Who said?

"Those who know, do. Those that understand, teach."

    a)   Plato
    b)   John F. Kennedy
    c)   Jaime Escalante
    d)   Aristotle

The answer is at the end of this chapter.

My story about the first time I taught in front of a classroom of students is a classic. But before I tell you about how I was able to turn a very embarrassing moment into a positive experience, I should probably start at the beginning and explain how and why I became a teacher in the first place.

I did not go to college to become a teacher. My college experience began in 1963 at Fairleigh Dickenson University (FDU) in Teaneck, New Jersey where I enrolled as an engineering major. I chose this school for two main reasons. One, is that it was only a one-hour drive from my parents' home. By being able to commute from home, I would not have to pay to live in a dorm or rent an apartment. The second is because my brother, Binnie (James), who was two years older than me, was also accepted to FDU as an engineering major. I was just seventeen years old and Binnie was nineteen.

Ever since I can remember, I have always been the youngest student in all of my grades. I'm not totally sure how that happened, but I remember that my parents once told me that I started first grade when I was five years old because my birthday was in April, the cutoff month for me to begin school.

I was not a great student in my early years but at the end of sixth grade, my parents were told that my reading and math levels were high enough to allow me to skip a grade and go straight to the eighth grade. Knowing that I was already one year younger than all my classmates, they did not think it would be fair to me, and they wisely declined.

Realizing that I had the capacity to do well in school did not help me become a better student. I was still emotionally immature and way too lazy to apply any innate skills. Somehow, I graduated high school with a "B" average, and a lot had to do with my grades in mathematics. Looking back, I am not proud to say that girls and sports were my high school major subjects nor am I proud to have the distinction of having the world's largest collection of undone homework assignments.

Being the youngest in my high school classes was tough enough, but when I got to college, it was even worse. One of the hardships I had to face as a freshman in college was that most of the girls were interested in "men." They had no interest in a seventeen-year-old baby. Dating for me was super difficult. In my four years of college, I probably set the *Guinness Book of Records* for the most blind dates. No, I wasn't ugly. I was just a kid among men. That and having the nicknames of "Brillo" and "Dumbo" did not help. Nicknames can be brutal, and they did they nothing for my self-esteem. I was okay with "Brillo" because my hair was not coarse, it was just curly and wavy. But "Dumbo" hurt. I also had another nickname. My aunt Marie's nickname for me was "Denny Dimwit."

Growing up with ears that stick out was not easy. My head looked like a taxicab with the doors left open. I remember going to bed at night and purposely lying down on my ears to flatten them out. Thirty minutes on the left ear then thirty minutes on the right ear. Yes, I really did this, and I did this night after night for about two years. It must have helped because my ears no longer stick out. *Yay!* Watch out, Brad Pitt.

Still, I can clearly remember during a college basketball game as I was dribbling up the court when a student sitting in the stands shouted, "Hey, Dumbo, can you fly?" Passive me wanted to punch him in the face with my elephant right hand.

To make college life even worse, if that was possible, I wasn't just the youngest student in my freshman class, I was also the most immature and laziest seventeen-year-old you even met. If it wasn't for my good grades in math, I don't think I would have made it to my college graduation.

The year my brother and I both started college, 1963, was an historically challenging year. On November 22, just a few months into the school year, President Kennedy was assassinated. My brother and I were both sitting in our 1:00 PM history class when we heard a student standing outside our room begin to shout, "President Kennedy has been shot." Our instructor quickly dismissed the class. Immediately upon leaving class, we raced to the parking lot to our car so we could drive the one-hour trip to our parents' home in Dobbs Ferry, New York. During that drive, as we were listening to the radio, we heard Walter Cronkite announce that our beloved president had died.

When we arrived home, we found our mom sitting on the couch crying uncontrollably as she was watching the TV news. As a Catholic, my mom took great pride in our president. She had nothing but love and admiration for this exceptional leader. You did not have to be a Catholic to admire this man. His tragic death was a painful loss to everyone not just in the United States but throughout the world. No one will ever forget where they were when they heard the terrible news.

In a few short months (February 1964), the Beatles would invade America. The radio hype for their arrival was insane. Instead of "The British are coming, the British are coming," the radio announcers were saying, "The Beatles are coming, the Beatles are coming." The Beatles trademark, of course, was their music, but they also had another and unique trademark: their bowl-cut hair. It was a very different hair style and most Americans were not used to it. It appeared to me that the young girls didn't care what kind of hair the Beatles had, or maybe it was their hair that helped perpetuate their mystique. On February 9th, it seemed like every American, and the rest of the world, was glued to their TV sets the night the Beatles appeared on the *Ed Sullivan Show.*

That night, on a whim, both my brother and I cut our hair in the style of the Beatles and went to our college classes the next day looking like members of the Beatles US fan club. This hairstyle worked a lot better for my brother because he had straight black hair. Not so for me with my curly and bushy brown hair (and my ears sticking out).

Let's flash forward a few years to May of 1967. Summer and graduation are fast approaching. I am barely twenty-one years old, and I will soon be graduating with a bachelor's degree in mathematics. What happened to engineering? Good question. All it took was one semester of college physics and my engineering career was over. Somehow, I managed to get a grade of "B" in physics, but I didn't earn it. My test average was an embarrassing, 53 percent. My brother, Binnie, received an "A" in physics, but he deserved his "A" with a 97 average.

After I finished my physics course, I began to wonder what kind of bridge would I be able to build with a 53-percent average? How long would it take before that bridge would surely collapse? Not wanting to be responsible for the deaths of hundreds of people, I quickly switched my major to mathematics.

It was obvious to me why science teachers curve their grades, but, as a teacher, I disagree with this practice. I believe that curving grades gives a false sense of accomplishment. There is no accomplishment in getting a 53-percent average. Math teachers, like myself, rarely, if ever, curve their grades. It's simple, if you get a 53 percent on a math test, your grade is an "F." Sorry.

As someone who was about to graduate college, I had one major problem. With just a few months to go, I still had no idea what I wanted to do with my life. Becoming a teacher was not a thought in my head. I did have a fantasy about being a sports statistician, but I never pursued it for a couple of reasons. For one, I was very idealistic and wanted to change the world and I couldn't quite do that as a sports statistician. Secondly, I also had fantasies of being a professional basketball player (stop laughing), which was way better than being a sports statistician.

However, becoming a pro athlete was not meant to be. Though I was good enough to play college basketball, my short height of 5'11" and inability to dribble a basketball (stop laughing), put an end to my basketball career. Fantasy over. I was proudly able to chalk up playing college basketball as a great experience. Little did I know at that time that my basketball shooting skills would eventually come in handy as a teacher.

As college graduation grew near, I remember being extremely envious of my friends who knew where their future was going. I would often think, *It's just not fair*. I was so very confused and lost. My guess is a lot of people reading this can identify with my feelings.

I was even envious of my brother who was also graduating with me. With a degree in engineering, he already had an offer from Grumman Aircraft to work on the Apollo Moon project. At least he knew what his immediate future would be. I am very proud to say that his name, Jame "Binnie" Rand (along with the other engineers), is on a plaque on the moon.

A few years later, Grumman lost its federal contract for the Apollo missions, and my brother was one of the unfortunate ones to get laid off. In the next six months, he went back to school and received a teaching license in mathematics and science. In 1970, after teaching for four years, I was able to pull some strings and get him a job as a math teacher in my school. Our students and colleagues affectionally knew us as K. Rand and J. Rand.

I was also envious of Binnie for another reason. He had a girlfriend. He was lucky enough to meet his future wife, the beautiful and intelligent Linda Sachs in our senior year of college. I was also in love. Her name was Ellen O'Brien. But, alas, it was one-sided. Don't worry, I got over it. It took two years, but I got over it. Now I can look back and laugh, but at that time, especially with my chronic low self-esteem, it was a tough time.

Ellen, if you are reading this, it wasn't your fault.

Things worked out OK. More than OK. I am now happily married for forty years (Vita) with two incredible sons (Kevin and Chris).

After fifty years of not hearing from each other, Ellen and I have reconnected and are friends on Facebook (which I rarely, if ever, go on).

I mentioned earlier how immature and unprepared I was when I enrolled in college. I hope the next chapter gives you some more insight to this flaw in my personality and study skills and you will soon learn how and why I became a teacher.

The answer is Aristotle.

Chapter Three

Dr. Davis

Extra credit: Who said?

"If we teach today's students as we taught yesterday's, we rob them of tomorrow."

- a) Ignacio "Nacho" Estrada
- b) John Dewey
- c) Benjamin Franklin
- d) Ken Rand

The answer is at the end of this chapter.

I have a great story that perfectly illustrates how bad a student I was in college. No, I am not bragging, I am more than embarrassed as to how lazy I was as a student and wish I could go back to school and start all over again.

As a freshman (1963) at Fairleigh Dickenson University in Teaneck, New Jersey, I, along with every other new college entry, were forced to take Freshman Economics 101 with Dr. Davis.

Dr. Davis was the only instructor for this course. He was also the only black professor on campus (remember this is 1963). He had a well-deserved reputation of being one of the most demanding professors on campus and not many students survived his course. He was, in fact, a great instructor, it's just that he was so intimidating.

Dr. Davis was in his early fifties, with thin, balding hair and had a light brown complexion. His most distinguishing feature, other than his mustache, was that he wore his glasses on the tip of his nose. He was also somewhat old-fashioned. He wore the same suit and tie every day and would often brag about his old beat-up 1949 Chevrolet that he drove to work every day. He would also frequently complain about the "extravagance" of purchasing needless items as a total waste of money. I clearly remember him say on a number of occasions, "Why, in the world, does anyone need five pairs of shoes?"

Dr. Davis never knew any of his students by name. He simply didn't care. If he wanted to ask a student a question, which he often did, he would look at his seating chart and call out your name.

DR. DAVIS, *looking at his seating chart*. Hmm? Mr. Rand, where are you?

ME, *raising my hand*. I'm here, Dr. Davis.

DR. DAVIS. Mr. Rand, could you explain to me, and the rest of the class, the economic concept of supply and demand?

Oh…I'm stuck. I didn't do my homework.

ME. I apologize, Dr. Davis, but I didn't have time to do my homework last night.

This was my first mistake.

DR. DAVIS. And why's that, Mr. Rand?

ME. I'm on the basketball team, and we didn't get off practice until about 7:00 PM last night. Then I had to go to Sears & Roebuck and work until 11:00 PM."

DR. DAVIS, *who was now walking toward me*. Mr. Rand, did you come to this college to play basketball or to get an education?

ME. Both.

This was my second mistake.

DR. DAVIS. Hmm? Mr. Rand, if you had to choose between playing basketball and receiving an education, then which would you choose?

I was hesitating, and this was my third mistake.

DR. DAVIS. Don't answer that, Mr. Rand, I have an answer for you.

With that he took out a dime and gave it to me.

ME. What's this for?

DR. DAVIS. I want you to call your mom and tell her to come pick you up from school and take you home. Tell her that I said that you were a worthless student and did not deserve to be here.

I was almost crying.

DR. DAVIS, *now inches from my face*. Tell her that you are a waste of space. Tell her it is unfair for her son to take the place of another student who would come here to learn.

I was sitting straight when this inquiry began, and now I am almost horizontal as if I am ready to be buried underground. Dr. Davis then started to walk back to his desk and after a few steps turned around and got right into my face again, and he was visibly angry.

DR. DAVIS. I am not finished with you yet, Mr. Rand.

And for the next fifteen minutes, he continued to destroy me and my character. *Wow, wow, wow!* You would think that I learned my lesson from this exchange, but nope, not me. I was just too immature (seventeen years old) and lazy. I promptly went on to fail the midterm exam. This put me in a rather tenuous position.

Dr. Davis only gave two exams, a midterm and a final. This meant that in order for me to pass this class with a grade of "C", I would have to ace the final exam. Not something that I was likely to do.

About three weeks before the final exam, Dr. Davis made this announcement to the class, "It seems that quite a few of you lazy freshman have failed my midterm exam. Because of this, I am going to give you one more chance to pass this class."

You could hear the knees shaking in the class.

DR. DAVIS, *continuing.* Your only chance to pass this class is to come to my SU.

A VERY BRAVE STUDENT. What's an SU, Dr. Davis?

DR. DAVIS. The SU is my personal *Size Up* of you. You are invited to come to my office on the morning of June 2nd where I will give you an oral final exam.

Not sure if you have ever taken an oral school exam for a course, but it is much more difficult than a "paper" test, and…you can't bull-shit your way out of it.

No choice. I had to go.

Dr. Davis' office was on the fourth floor of an old Victorian home. This beautiful old building had a winding staircase (and, of course, no elevator). When I arrived at the building, there was a line of over fifty students waiting their turn to take the oral exam. There was so many of us that Dr. Davis decided to take 5–7 of us at a time.

It was a frightening scene. Students were walking back down the stairs in tears after taking his oral exam. We were asking them about the exam, but they were too shook up to talk. Some of them looked like they were about to throw up. This did not look good. It was kind of like waiting outside a dentist office and hearing patients scream in pain before it was your turn to go in (and thanks to Dr. Rosen, our family dentist, these were sounds that I was only to familiar with).

After about two hours of waiting on the staircase, there were now only seven of us left. Dr. Davis came out of his office and looked us over and told all seven of us to come in (and he wasn't smiling).

So, here's the scene. The seven of us were in a huge attic-type room with a vaulted ceiling. Dr. Davis was sitting at a desk that looked like it was a hundred years old, and we were lined up about 10 feet away. It looked and felt like the infamous Saturday night massacre from the Al Capone story.

Dr. Davis said, "I'm tired, so I have only one question for all of you. Each of you will take a turn in answering the question and be prepared to back up your answer with sound economic reasoning. Here is your question. There seems to be a surplus of food in the United States, and my simple question to you is what would you do with it? Remember to back up your answer with sound economic reasoning."

One by one, each of the students would try to sound ultrasmart and talk about supply and demand and how they would either destroy the food or store it for a later day. It finally became my turn to offer my words of wisdom.

ME. Dr. Davis, I would give the food away.

DR. DAVIS, *with a quizzical look.* Hmm? You look very familiar. What's your name, son?

Oh shit, he remembered me. I'm dead. It's over.

ME, *visibly shaking and in my lowest voice.* Myy nammme is Ken Rand.

DR. DAVIS. I knew you looked familiar. This should be fun. Tell me, Mr. Rand, why would you give the food away?

ME, *still shaking.* Dr. Davis, there are people in the United States who are homeless and hungry. It doesn't make sense to destroy or store the food.

DR. DAVIS. Hmm? Interesting, but can you back it up with sound economic reasoning?

35

ME. I thought for a minute and said, "no, I'm sorry, Dr. Davis. It just seems like the right thing to do."
DR. DAVIS, *looking around at the other students.* Would any of you like to argue with Mr. Rand and punch holes in his answer?

One by one each of the students stuck to their guns about "supply and demand" and how giving away food for free would not be a sound economic solution.

DR. DAVIS. Mr. Rand, I am going to give you one more chance. Either change your answer or back it up with economic reasoning.
ME. Dr. Davis, I will not change my answer.
DR. DAVIS. Why, and don't give me crap about people being hungry.

I thought for a brief moment and finally said, "Dr. Davis, if you feed hungry people, then they will be healthier. If people are healthy, then they can go to work. If they go to work, they can make money. If they make money, then they can spend money. If they spend money, they are helping the economy."

DR. DAVIS. You are all dismissed.

I walked out of that room shaking like a leaf. Usually walking down a staircase was easier than walking up a staircase, but not this time. All I could do now was wait for my grade, which I was sure was going to be an "F."

A week later, I received all my grades in the mail. I could not wait until I saw my grades for economics. I was totally shocked when I saw that I received a "B" for the year. End of story.

The answer is John Dewey.

Chapter Four

Dancin' Machine

Who said the following:

"Courage is not the absence of fear, but the ability to overcome it."

    a)   Jackie Robinson
    b)   John Glenn
    c)   Ken Rand (me)
    d)   Nelson Mandela

The answer is at the end of this chapter.

I have a little side story that happened in our senior year in college, and hope you'll enjoy it.

Both my brother Binnie and I loved to dance. We were brought up with music. Neither one of us were musically gifted like our dad, but we both excelled in dancing. Each summer, our dad would take us to Brown's Hotel in the Catskill Mountains in upstate New York where my dad was the musical director and band leader. During those summer months, Binnie and I would practice dance routines to the Latin music of the cha-cha, the mambo, and the merengue. The hotel had three bands, a show band, a rock band, and a Latin band.

Binnie and I eventually became good enough to even dance professionally on the weekly Wednesday Mambo Night in the Catskills. We were also pretty good at contemporary dancing, and the Lindy Hop was still the dance style of the day, and we were both really good about improvising our own unique and interesting freestyle dance moves.

Anyway, while we were in our senior year at college, we were invited, on a Friday afternoon, to a local TV dance show, and we went there with about sixteen other college friends. Each week, this show had a dance contest which we were all well aware of. Binnie was with his future wife, Linda, and I was with my regular dance partner, Marney.

On the drive down to the TV studio, Binnie leaned over to me and whispered in my ear, "Do you mind if we switch dance partners?"

Surprised, I asked him, "Why?"

He was honest and said, "I think I have a better chance of winning the contest with your partner."

I thought about it for a minute and asked him, "Does Linda know?"

He said, "Not yet."

I smiled and wondered how she would take this news. I am pretty competitive, and I also wanted to win, but I was also very confident in both Linda and I, and I told him, "Okay, we'll switch. Good luck."

There were at least twenty other couples on the dance floor when the contest started. Remember, this was on TV, so it was kind of a big deal. If you were tapped on the shoulder by a judge, it meant that you had to leave the dance floor. One by one, the other couples left the floor, and as fate would have it, it was now down to two couples: Binnie and my original partner, Marney, and me with Binnie's future wife, Linda.

Guess who won? To my brother's great disappointment, Linda and I won. Thank you, Linda. You made me look good. Funny thing is that I don't remember what the first-place prize was. I guess beating my brother was good enough for me (and especially for Linda).

I hope you enjoyed this side story. Back to my confusion about my future.

The answer is Nelson Mandela.

Chapter Five
Uncle Meyer to the Rescue

Who said the following:

"Teaching is the greatest act of optimism."

- a) Coleen Wilcox
- b) LouAnne Johnson
- c) Michelle Obama
- d) Oprah Winfrey

The answer is at the end of this chapter.

About a month before graduation, a representative from the Peace Corps (an international program originated by President John F. Kennedy and Pierre Salinger) came to the Fairleigh Dickenson campus. The more I thought about it, the more the Peace Corps seemed to be a fit for me, especially since I did not have a job waiting for me when I graduated. *Hmmm?* I also thought that traveling to a foreign country would be a great experience.

With that in mind, I impulsively signed up. The Corps soon had me take some of their tests and, based on the results, assigned me to a teaching post in Kenya. Time was moving rather quickly, too quickly, and I had only one month after my graduation to get ready to fly to Kenya, Africa.

I am not sure why I didn't tell my dad right away about my new job with the Peace Corps. Maybe I kind of knew what his reaction would be. Well, with only one week to go before I was off to Kenya, I finally told him about the assignment. It's now June of '67.

After the shock wore off, my dad confronted me with twenty-one questions, the most important of which was "Why?" I told him that I wasn't sure about my future and that I was thinking about being a sports statistician. I went on to tell him that being a statistician didn't quite fit in with my desire to change the world. He then looked at me with his wise and proud eyes, smiled, and said, "You can change the world right here, why go to Africa?"

He went on to say, "Instead of teaching in Africa, you can teach here (in Westchester County, New York), or if not here then maybe in New York City."

At that time, we lived only about 20 miles from the city. I must admit that he had a good point. But there was a minor problem, I did not have a teaching license, a detail that the Peace Corps did not care about.

One of my dad's best friends, Meyer Packer (Uncle Meyer), called me the next day. Meyer was a junior high school music teacher in New York City and an adjunct instructor at City University in New York (CUNY). During that call, Meyer told me about a special summer program at the City University Education College where I could get my master's degree in math/education plus a teaching license for free. The word "free" sounded pretty good to me. I had no real knowledge about City University but quickly found out that it is a huge multi-college campus on Convent Avenue and 138th street near Harlem in Manhattan.

The trade-off for getting a free master's degree was that I'd be willing to sacrifice two years of my professional life and teach in the New York City public school system. In 1967, there was a tremendous shortage of teachers in New York City, perhaps even nationwide, especially in math and science. The city was desperate, and this new program was a result of that desperation. Veteran teachers even had a name for those of us who enrolled and graduated in this summer program. They called us the "sixty-day wonders."

There wasn't much time to think it over because the program was going to start in one week. I quickly filled out the application forms, and I was beginning to look forward to graduate school and the possibility of becoming a teacher. There was tremendous time pressure, but I managed to do the necessary paperwork and pass the required exams, including the grueling and difficult five-hour graduate record exam (GRE).

It all happened so fast, but I was accepted to City University graduate school and planned to major in math/education. Sadly, I found my summer graduate courses in education to be boring (I really mean *borrring*). And I am being way too polite when I say "boring."

Our graduate school instructors knew that we were on a conveyor belt to get a teaching license and the necessary education units, so they just tried to zip in as much knowledge and theory as possible into an eight-week summer session. Staying awake in those classes was quite a challenge. My graduate instructors were a great example of the kind of teacher that I did not want to be.

Within a few weeks, I would soon find out what kind of teacher I was meant to be. Get ready to laugh out loud.

The answer is Coleen Wilcox.

Chapter Six
My First Day

Who said the following:

"Education is not the filling of a pail, but the lighting of a fire."

    a)   Emily Dickenson
    b)   William Butler Yeats
    c)   Carl Sanders
    d)   Robert Frost

The answer is at the end of this chapter.

All of us who participated in the sixty-day summer master's program was assigned to student teach in a New York City school for two weeks near the end of summer. My assignment was to observe and teach at a junior high school (middle school) on 123rd Street in Harlem, New York. During that assignment, there was a very memorable and embarrassing experience.

Each day, for two weeks, I took the forty-five-minute commute to my assigned school in Harlem. The contrast between living in Westchester with its beautiful tree-lined streets and hills and the gray, very gray, extremely gray streets and buildings of Manhattan was stark.

Every day during the first week, I would sit in the back of the classroom, observing my supervising mentor teacher. It was extremely uncomfortable for a variety of reasons. There was a terrible heat wave that week, it was sweltering hot and horribly humid. No air conditioning and no fan. The combination of the heat, humidity, and having over thirty students in a stuffy room made for a physically unpleasant environment. Having the classroom windows opened did not seem to make any difference.

As I sat in the back of that room, sweating, I would try not to daydream, and forced myself to take notes while my supervisor expertly taught his eighth-grade summer school math class. I can recall feeling extremely nervous and feared the inevitable moment that I would be asked to teach the class.

As each day went by, I found myself continually waiting for that dreadful day and hoping my teaching mentor (who was an excellent teacher) would hopefully forget I was even there. The words "Okay! The class is yours" were words I just was not ready to hear.

I spent the entire first week doing my best to simply focus on his style with the hope of learning something, anything, about how to teach. My education courses at City University did not teach me how to teach.

Well that day finally came, and it came without warning or prior notice. My supervising teacher came to up me right before class started on Monday and said, "Today's the day. You're taking over. I'll sit in the back and observe. Just be yourself." *Ha, easy for him to say!*

He then went in front of the class and announced, "Mr. Rand is going to be your teacher today and for the rest of the week. Today he is going to teach you how to reduce fractions. I want you to show him the same respect that you show me. Be on your best behavior. I will still be here, sitting in the back of the room."

My brain was saying, *Thank you, thank you, thank you.*

I am very good (really good) at reducing fractions. I can reduce fractions in my sleep, but I was totally clueless as to how to teach it. You need to remember that this was about fifty years ago. There wasn't any Internet, no overhead projectors, no power points, etc. And no prior preparation. Just nervous me and a blackboard, white chalk, and an eraser (thank, God, for erasers).

As a reader, I want you to imagine how you might feel if you went to work on your first day knowing you have had the sum total of zero training for your job. It is beyond frightening, it's terrifying. *Okay, this patient has a brain tumor go ahead and operate.* Or *Your job is to create the backup fail-safe electrical system for the Apollo spacecraft. Good luck. Don't worry, but their lives depend upon your success. Just be yourself.*

As a teacher, we are responsible for educating hundreds of students and to teach them what we already know how to do. The ability to transfer knowledge is a gift. It is an art. Again, imagine trying to do this without any training. *Good luck!*

So here I am, standing in front of a classroom of students for the first time in my life. In an effort to try to look older and more professional, I chose to wear a new suit. Not a good choice.

The heat wave was still hovering over New York City—and it was around 97 degrees with an equal amount of humidity. Because of the heat, I took off my suit jacket, and that was a mistake. My armpits were sweating a river, and the sweat stains were showing on my light blue dress shirt (not cool at all). I am sure that I would have still sweated even if it was 10 degrees outside.

Before I even had a chance to say something stupid, my hands started nervously shaking. While getting ready to write my name on the board and simultaneously searching for some profound words of wisdom, I accidentally dropped a few pieces of chalk out of my hand onto the floor. There were a few snickers from some students, but it was not too bad. Not yet.

When I bent down to pick up the chalk, some of the pens in my shirt pocket also fell to the floor. So now I had to bend over for a second time. The giggling now turned into laughter. I haven't even said "Hi" yet, and I am already making a fool out of myself.

It gets worse. Much worse.

Now I am bending over to pick up the chalk and the pens, and my pants (brand-new suit slacks) ripped right on my big butt. Oh my god. I'm laughing to myself right now because my wife tells me that my butt disappeared forty years ago.

Anyway, the students all started to laugh hysterically. I was incredibly embarrassed. I didn't know what to do or say. I wanted to hide and disappear. Unfortunately for me, I was too big to hide under a desk, so that was no good.

Somehow, through divine guidance, I was mentally quick. I immediately stood up, turned to look at the rip in my butt, and with a straight face, I said to the class on this extremely hot day, "Thank God for air-conditioning." And then all thirty students, in unison, laughed and continued to laugh for the next five minutes (seemed like an hour to me). My supervising teacher was bent over laughing, and he almost fell off his chair. Even I had to laugh at my own joke and awkwardness.

But it was at that moment that I had them. It didn't matter that I was about to pedagogically botch this lesson. I soon relaxed, regained my composure, and just became myself. My supervisor was right. It really could not get any worse. The students didn't care what I was about to teach them. They now trusted me. I was now a real person to them. I unintentionally allowed myself to be vulnerable. It was either that or they were all waiting for me to embarrass myself again.

I began to show them, with a constant breeze on my butt, the technique I used to reduce fractions. I quickly realized, however, that they did not have the multiplication skills needed to do it "my way." I then tried to make it easier for them. I realized that I needed to look at the math problems the way that they were looking at them. The students were very patient and listened to every word I said. By the way, for you, future teachers, don't practice ripping your pants in front of your students on the first day. It's too expensive and way too embarrassing.

At the end of the class, my supervisor walked up to me and silently stared. I looked at him and said, "Wow, I really botched it, huh?" and then he said, "Don't worry about your future. Either you are a born comedian or born to be a great teacher."

For the next four days of my short student teaching career, the students were on the edge of their seats, waiting for me to embarrass myself again, and I tried very hard to keep bending over to a minimum. I also went on a diet.

What was also very clear to me at that time is that my education courses at City University did nothing to prepare me for the real world, the real classroom. There was way too much theory, way too much reading. Not enough role playing, not enough creativity. Boring. Boring. And the two weeks of student teaching was not nearly enough practice. Two years would have been much better.

One of the other things I learned that week was the concept of "making it simple" for my students. This thought became an important theme throughout my entire career as a teacher.

At the end of the summer, I finished my education courses and passed the appropriate tests. Within a week, I quickly received my New York State teaching license. I still needed eighteen more units for my master's degree, which I would eventually receive.

There was still one major hurdle, I now needed a job.

The answer to the opening quote is William Butler Yeats.

Chapter Seven
Unio Igh 125

Extra credit: Who said?

"True teachers are those who use themselves as bridges over which they invite their students to cross; then, having facilitated their crossing, joyfully collapse, encouraging them to create their own."

    a)   Nikos Kazantzakis
    b)   Rita Pearson
    c)   Kenneth Temsky
    d)   Dr. Ken Harris

The answer is at the end of this chapter.

Once again, Uncle Meyer came to the rescue. Meyer had a friend who was a principal at a junior high school in the Bronx, and he helped set me up for my first teaching interview. That friend was Dr. Ralph Freyer, principal of Junior High School 125 in the south Bronx. The name of the school, "Henry Hudson," was displayed in large two-foot brass letters on the top of the school entrance. Evidently, over time, some of the letters and numbers fell off the facade and under the name of the school stood the remaining letters, "Henry Hudson Unio Igh 125."

Below is a more recent photo of the school. It looks like they repaired the fallen letters.

There's only about one week left before the end of summer, and schools will soon be open for the next school year. Here I am, twenty-one years old, I have never had a formal job interview in my life and I never had a full-time job. The drive from my parent's home in Dobbs Ferry, New York, to the school in the Southeast Bronx took only about thirty minutes, and during that entire trip I was mentally rehearsing the possible interview questions and answers that were just minutes away from reality.

As I was walking up the steps to enter the school, I tripped, but luckily, I was able to catch my balance. Another good thing is that no one saw it. I started to tell myself, *Focus. Focus.* I was so nervous, too nervous. As I walked into the school, I could see the General Office immediately on my right. I walked in and was ready for the unexpected. Well, I wasn't ready enough.

When I walked into the office, the administrative assistant mistook me for a student, a rather well-dressed student, she said, "Summer school grades are in the mail. You'll just have to wait like anyone else."

Confused, I said, "I am here for an interview with Dr. Freyer."

Without as much even glancing at me, she went over to his office, which was a few feet away, and shouted with her Bronx accent, "D'yu have an interview now?"

His office door was open, and I could hear him shout, "Send him in!"

Mr. Freyer was sitting behind his desk in his smoke-filled office and was puffing on a cigar. Even though he was sitting down, I could see that Dr. Freyer was rather short, probably about 5'6". His face was wrinkled, showing the effects of too many years of smoking. The combination of all those years of smoking and his mustache made him look like a one-hundred-year-old Groucho Marx. For you, millennials, you'll just have to google "Groucho Marx."

He started the interview by shouting at me (with the door open), "So why do you want to teach, and don't give me any of that liberal bullshit."

He didn't even greet me. He didn't say "Hello" or "Have a seat," no pleasantries at all. Right now, I am really laughing out loud, but at that time, it wasn't so funny.

Again, I was only twenty-one years old, this was my first interview ever. I wasn't even in his office one minute and he was already trying to intimidate me. I had been prewarned by Uncle Meyer that Dr. Freyer had a reputation of being an "intimidator," but he also said that Freyer's bite was worse than his bark. I'm not sure I wanted to find out.

You won't believe the answer I naively gave him. I looked right at him, even though he was not looking back at me, and said, "Dr. Freyer, I was born to teach." This was probably the first and last time, over a ten-year period, that I ever heard him laugh. He didn't just laugh, like my student teaching supervisor, he almost fell out of his chair. Now I'm thinking, *Maybe I really should be a comic?*

Sorry for the diversion, but this story just reminded me of a postcard I received from a former student. He was a student of mine in 1998 while I was teaching in California. I received the postcard from him in 2004. The postcard was postmarked from New York City. Here's what he said,

Hi Mr. Rand,

How are you? I just wanted to thank you for helping get through your math course. I also wanted to let you know that you have inspired me like no other teacher I have ever had. I never would have

*achieved my dreams without you. Thanks again
and take care.*

*PS Right now I am a stand-up comic in New
York City*

This postcard gave me a great laugh. All I could think of is
that someone is using all my classroom jokes and now making more
money than I am.

Back to the interview.

Freyer's question and his tone took me off guard. I just didn't
know what else to say. All I could think of at the time was to repeat
to him something that my summer student teacher supervisor said
about me.

After he stopped laughing at me, Freyer's next question was, "If
I hire you, please tell me you're not going to go on strike with those
other idiots."

This question I had prepared for because the newspapers had
daily articles about the pending New York City teacher's strike. I lied
and told him that I wasn't really sure and I still needed to give it some
thought. I already knew that if I was hired, I would go on strike and
honor my new colleagues.

Freyer's smile soon turned to a frown, and he shouted at me,
"You're lucky that I am desperate. You're hired. Now get out of my
office and go see my assistant."

The whole interview lasted less than five minutes. And that was
it. He hired me on the spot. He must have been really desperate. All
the rehearsing that I did was a waste of time. This was not a formal
interview. It was a lesson in intimidation.

The administrative assistant called me over to her desk and
gave me my teaching schedule for the upcoming school year. I was
given five math classes. Two seventh-grade classes (7N, 7W), one
eighth grade (8T), and two ninth-grade algebra classes (9H and 9G).
Confused by the alphabetical designations of my classes, I asked her,
"What's does 7N and the other letters mean?" She told me that it

was just the way the school distinguished one class from the other. I would soon find out that this was only a half truth.

She also told me that my 7N math class would also be my "homeroom" class and that I would meet with them each morning from 8:00 to 8:30 and take attendance and go over any announcements. I was also to meet them at the end of the day from 2:45 to 3:00 to take attendance again. She told me that she was very busy and called over a student monitor to show me around the school.

The school was huge. It had three floors, and there was a basement with a cafeteria. There was no way that I would remember any details during this short tour. It was all kind of overwhelming to me. Also, as we were walking, my mind was too focused on the names of my students as I was reading my class rosters. There is no doubt that I would probably get lost in this school at least one hundred times before I was able to find my way around.

The inevitable teacher's strike (organized by the American Federation of Teachers led my Albert Shanker) did happen, and it lasted two weeks. Ouch! No salary for two weeks. This really hurt my already empty wallet. The next year, it was even worse, the New York City teacher's union went on strike for nine weeks.

My decision to support my colleagues by going on strike with them, no one would have blamed me if I didn't, was a good one. Walking the picket line with them helped me bond with my fellow teachers. This is extremely important for a first-year teacher.

During the strike, the New York City teacher's union set up learning centers throughout the city called "street academies." I was feeling the "teacher's guilt" and really had nothing else to do except walk the picket line at the school, so I decided to work in one of the street academies.

Contrary to popular opinion, teacher's do not want to go on strike. Many of my colleagues who backed the strike were equally concerned about our students missing precious days of school. This reluctance to strike because of this concern is what I call "teacher's guilt."

However, the overriding factor that New York City teachers were the lowest-paid teachers of any major city in the country far outweighed our guilty conscience. I should also add that public school administrators found too many ways to allow average class sizes to be around forty students per class even though the current contract only permitted thirty-two students per class.

There was also overwhelming public support for the strike, and about 98 percent of all New York City teachers supported the strike by walking the picket lines. The schools tried to hire substitutes (scabs) to take our place, but only of handful of them were willing to cross the picket lines. I can remember that there were a lot of "army" curses shouted at them while they tried to go into the school. This scene would have been definitely been rated an "R."

The street academy which I taught at was in the basement of a nearby church. Again, I had no idea how to teach, but teaching in this off-school location was a great learning experience. I had no choice but to try my best. I flirted with the idea of telling my students that this was my first teaching job, hoping and looking for empathy, but there was also this voice in my head that said that this would not be a good idea.

So, for the next two weeks, I continued to fake it. These few weeks that I taught in the church school also turned out to be a good decision for me for another reason. Even though I didn't know what I was doing, the students were very respectful, and they kind of took to me. I was told by my colleagues that most of students who attended the academies were some of the better students whose parents had a deeper concern for education.

Each day, after the classes were over, I would play basketball with a small group of students in the church's gymnasium. Having previously played college basketball, I was more than able to hold my own, which was kind of easy because they were all much shorter than me. "Yo, Teach, you can really shoot for a white guy."

The strike was now over, and just for a perspective, my first regular paycheck after the strike was for $250, and it was a two-week paycheck. Do the math.

I probably should tell you something about the demographics of the school. Located in the Southeast Bronx, it was a multicultural school where it was evenly split with about 30 percent black, 30 percent Puerto Rican, 30 percent white, and about 10 percent other. The neighborhoods near the school weren't all that bad, but more than half of the students in the school were bused in from another part of the Bronx called Hunts Point.

Hunts Point is a place that I should be familiar with because I was born in Hunts Point Hospital. Unfortunately, I don't remember a thing about the hospital or Hunts Point. My family did not live there, and our apartment, which was over a laundromat, was on Cypress Ave and 138th Street and about a mile away.

For those of you who do not know anything about Hunts Point, especially in the 1960s, the best explanation I can give you is that at that time in history, Hunts Point was known as the drug capital of New York City.

My "real" first day is now one day away. I have no real teacher training, no real experience. And I would soon find out what was meant by the designations of 7N, 7W, etc.

The answer is Nikos Kazantzakis.

Chapter Eight
"Sit Down. Sit Down"

Extra credit: Who said?

"We never know which lives we influence, or when, or why?

a)   Bill Gates
b)   Steven Dawkins
c)   Stephen King
d)   Melissa Gates

The answer is at the end of this chapter.

When the strike was over, we all went back to our jobs at our schools, a lot of the students who were in my new classes remembered me from the street academy school. This was a good thing because some of them would bring their friends up to me and tell them, "This 'teach' is really cool, and he can really play ball." I also found out that my new name was "Teach"! This name just came with the territory and was not meant to be disrespectful. It was extremely rare for a student to call me by my name, "Mr. Rand."

My first day of "real" teaching was surprisingly uneventful. There was just so much to do. I had to take attendance, hand out textbooks, give out a seating arrangement, etc. It would be great to makeup some wild story about how I saved a student's life by breaking up a fight, but I really don't remember much about that first day. Maybe the drugs had taken effect. Just kidding. I'm not a druggie.

However, it wasn't unusual for a few of my contemporary colleagues to come to school just a wee bit high. Remember, this was the '60s.

The students in the school had somewhat of a hierarchy in terms of age and behavior. My seventh graders were as new to the school as I was. Being the youngest students in the school, they had yet to learn the ropes and were somewhat passive. Being young and somewhat timid, many of them had cute personalities.

Eighth graders were a totally different story. It was as if their hormones took over them during their summer, and they were now aware (too much aware) of the opposite sex. Ask any New York City junior high school teacher, and they will unanimously tell you that eighth graders are the most difficult grade to handle in terms of discipline.

Ninth graders weren't too bad. They knew that this was their last year here and were looking forward to graduating and going on to high school.

As mentioned in my previous chapter, I was assigned to teach the following math classes, 7N, 7W, 8T, 9G, and 9H. You probably now have the same questions that I had. Though it was obvious to me that the numbers were the grade levels, I had no idea what the letters (N, W, etc.) meant. I was soon told by other instructors that somehow the administrative gods thought it would be best to have the students grouped homogeneously using a combination of their reading and math levels. In elementary schools, students are grouped heterogeneously. There are no "smart" classes or "dumb" classes for these elementary grades.

In our junior high school, those students who had the highest reading and math levels in the seventh grade went into classes designated as 7A, 7B, or 7C and likewise for the eighth and ninth grades. When I found out the meaning of the letters, I was both puzzled and upset. This method of classifying and sorting students was very disturbing to me for many reasons.

It is very easy to figure out that the students in classes like 7N, 7W, and 8T had reading and math levels way below their grade level. This system made it a challenge for any instructor, especially a first-year instructor. It was difficult not to get caught up in predetermining or the stereotyping of the skills and attitudes and behaviors of our students. I can only imagine what students in 8T thought about themselves. My guess is that they probably thought that they were "dumb." I simply can't imagine what it would feel like knowing that you were going into a "dumb" class.

To me, I did not look at my students as "bright" or "dumb." I resisted the natural tenancy to do this. I know it sounds corny, but to me they all had unlimited potential. One thing was for sure, the students in the higher alphabet class designations, such as 8T, also brought with them a myriad of behavior problems which brings up the second thing that bothered me.

Most of the veteran instructors had teaching schedules where they taught the students in the A–E classes, and new teachers, like me, were given students in classes from N–Z. I understand the "seniority" system, but in this case, it was a pedagogical inconsistency, and it backfired.

Think about it for a minute. The students who needed the most help, those with the lower reading and math levels and those who were most likely to be behavior problems, were given to "rookie" or novice instructors like me. However, rookies like myself knew little or nothing about teaching, reaching, and managing students. Meanwhile, the veteran instructors, because of their teaching experience, were, in practicality, the teachers who were best prepared to work with and help these students. They are the teachers who should have been assigned to teach the more difficult students. The veteran and experienced instructors were able to escape these problems by teaching the well-behaved and academically brighter students in the better classes. *Hmm?* Didn't make sense then and doesn't make sense now.

I was new, and I was told to keep my mouth shut, but that would not last too long. At the first faculty meeting, I got the courage to stand up and ask Dr. Freyer, "Do our students know the meaning of the alphabet letters when they are placed into their classes?"

Tony Falbo, an English teacher who was sitting next to me, looked at me like I was crazy and said in a whisper "Sit down, sit down."

I quickly sat down. My question was ignored and never answered. But it became obvious. The students knew what the "letters" meant.

Give me a break. Anyone ever hear of a self-fulfilling prophecy? Was I the only teacher that saw the injustice and stigmatization of this system? I soon made it a personal goal to have this system changed. Why should I sit down? I know right from wrong even if I am a rookie teacher.

About a month later, at the next staff meeting, I got up again to ask the same question. Falbo, who is now my buddy, looked at me and whispered again, "Sit down, Rand!" This time I kept on standing.

I said, "Why can't we use the room numbers to designate our classes, like 7-201 or 8-153, instead of using the alphabet system?"

Freyer, the principal, gave me a dirty look. He said, "Then how are teachers supposed to know the level of the students?"

I said, "It's simple, let's make the classes heterogeneous. Let's mix up those with high reading and math levels with those with low levels." I almost got booed out of the meeting.

What you need to know is that my idea would cause a lot of extra work for the teachers and administrators. It was much easier to teach students if they were all on the same level. Though this is true, somehow, I stirred up the pot, and guess what happened the next school year? The administration compromised. They kept the classes homogenous but changed the class designation using room numbers, such as 7-201 etc. A moral *victory*! One windmill at a time.

As a first-year teacher, I was determined to make it my goal to visit many of the homes of my students, especially those who lived in Hunts Point. This not only helped me develop a rapport with my students and their families, but it also gave me firsthand knowledge of the miserable, unsettling, and dangerous lives that some of my students, and their families, were living. I also remember being anxious and scared while walking through the Hunts Point neighborhood.

This was not fear caused by any stereotyping, this was real fear. Quite often, in my first year of teaching, while visiting their homes, three or four of my students would walk me to my car (an orange convertible Volkswagen bug), and there was always a student's brother or friend watching over my car while I was having dinner with their family.

Every time I drove home, I would think, *I have to do something to change their lives.* It became who I was. I could quickly see that the combinations of poverty, drugs, and a single-parent home were the main reasons for our students failing.

I became determined to be someone who would make a difference in the lives of my students. Someone who would give them hope. Someone who would give them confidence. Someone who would show them a future other than the one they thought they were destined to live. I didn't it realize yet, but I needed to do this, one student at a time.

The Answer is Steven King.

Chapter Nine

"Randdd. . .Rannnddd. . .where is he?"

Extra credit: Who said?

"The teacher who walks in the shadow of the temple, among his followers, gives not of his wisdom but rather of his faith and his lovingness."

   a)   Rene Descartes
   b)   Steven Dawkins
   c)   Thoreau
   d)   Khalil Gibran

The answer is at the end of this chapter.

"Randdd...RANNNDDD! Where's is he?" That's my principal, Dr. Ralph Freyer, shouting out of his office into the hallways of our junior high school in the Bronx, New York.

My classroom was just a short distance away, and I was teaching my seventh-grade math class. My door was open when this outburst erupted from his office.

This incident happened after about three months into my rookie year of teaching. This was the first of many confrontations when Freyer had an issue with me. Quickly after this outburst, Freyer sent a student monitor to drag me out of my class. When I got to his office, I immediately started to cough as a reaction to his cigar smoke.

He didn't waste any time and shouted at me, "What's this crap I hear about you playing Monopoly in the classroom?" Before I could answer, he gave me the hairy eyeball and said, "Rand, you aren't here to play games and have fun, you're here to teach. Don't you understand that?"

Again, I was just twenty-one years old, a very young teaching rookie, and Freyer took immense pleasure in trying to intimidate me. *Hmmm? Having fun and learning at the same time. What a novel approach? So much for innovation?*

Not knowing what to say to the "intimidator" but wanting to continue with the Monopoly game going on in my class, I told him, "Dr. Freyer, with all due respect, you probably need to come and see my class in action before you yell at me again."

He then sarcastically said, "Sorry to hurt your feelings, Rand."

I ignored that comment and just motioned to him and asked him to follow me to my classroom where the monopoly "math" was in full swing.

Freyer then shouted, "I've got better things to do than follow you to your class."

I gave up and went back to my classroom. A few minutes later, he finally came to my classroom and walked around, carefully eyeing the students who were all sitting in small groups. The desks were rearranged so that five or six students would better be able to communicate together.

Meanwhile the Monopoly game board was leaning on the blackboard in front of the class in full view for all students. Each group was their own real estate company which they self-named as corporations, such as the "Hunts Point Co-Op" or "Bronx International LLP." They also self-appointed a student in their group to be the CEO and another student as the groups' treasurer.

Freyer continued to walk around my classroom, talking to the students, asking them questions, and all the while he had this angry look on his face. He always looked angry. It appeared to me that he was looking for some reason to fire me. While Freyer was walking around, my students were excitedly engaged in making decisions as to which property they either wanted to buy or trade, and they were "doing the math." They were learning the basic math skills of whole numbers, fractions, and percent, but this time, they were having fun. Engaging my students in their own learning process became just one of the many teaching themes that I carried with me throughout my teaching career.

Freyer just continued to walk around the class, growling like an angry cat, and then he suddenly walked out of the room and slammed my door. That was it. He never said anything more to me about it again. It looked like I lived to teach another day.

For the record, the game lasted for about two weeks. The winning team of the classroom Monopoly received free movie tickets from me. After the two-week game was over, I also gave my students a Monopoly test. If one house cost $135, then how much was four houses, etc. How much was 15 percent of $2,000? This game was just the beginning of my attempts to try to get creative in the classroom.

What made me decide to bring Monopoly into my classroom? There are a couple of reasons. One of them is because I was tired of writing failed lesson plans. Nowhere in any of my education courses did it tell me the importance of connecting and engaging with students. Nor was I taught the necessity of making learning relevant to our students.

I was bored and confused writing useless lesson plans, and you can just imagine my students' feelings when they tried to follow my somewhat less than brilliant approach to teaching fractions. How do you write a lesson plan for something that you have never taught before? How do you even know where to begin?

I became obsessed with becoming creative. I loved to play games at home with my family, including scrabble, chess, monopoly, and mastermind. One night after playing monopoly, with my family, I saw the essential and basic mathematics needed to play this game. I had a big family. There were seven of us. Mom, Dad, my oldest brother, Frankie, then my brother Binnie, my sister Judy was a year younger than me, and my brother Johnny was twelve years younger than me.

One night, while we were playing Monopoly, I had an "Ah ha" moment, and I came up with the idea of using Monopoly as a teaching tool in my lower level seventh- and eighth-grade classes. And... it worked. The concept of a 15 percent tax was part of the monopoly game, but this time when I taught percentages, I had the eyes and ears and minds of all my students.

Multiplication and word problems became a wanted necessity of knowledge to my students. The concept of working as corporations in groups and working as a team became invaluable. Not sure when collaborative learning became an effective educational classroom tool, but it was obvious to me, even as a first-year teacher that "two heads were better than one." I was very proud of myself even if it meant almost getting fired.

This teaching success led me to teach my students how to play chess (the best thinking game ever created), and I also taught them how to play a game called "Mastermind," which is a great game of logical thinking. My seventh-grade developmental students, for the first time, in their very short educational careers, were learning how to think, and they were having fun being engaged in their own learning process.

Frank McCourt, the author of *Teacher Man*, Aric Bostic (a gifted education speaker), and other great teachers, such as Kim Thomas, Patricia Garcia, Greg Perkins, Kim Tobey, Johnny Perez, Jim Butler, and countless of other teachers, had to find that out the hard way. By that, I mean that we did it on our own, not only as a means for survival but with a profound desire to change the lives of our students. So, the combination of storytelling, making learning relevant and fun, and engaging our students became a necessity to have successful teaching.

The answer is Khalil Gibran.

Chapter Ten
Jacque Dawes

Who said?

"Each day we are born with a gift and an opportunity. The gift is life itself. The opportunity is to make a difference is someone else's life."

- a) Aristotle
- b) Albert Einstein
- c) Jaime Escalante
- d) Ken Rand (me)

The answer is at the end of this chapter.

Jacque Dawes

Michael Hadley (chapter 1) was definitely a great example of why teachers teach. Here's another story from my first year of teaching that speaks to that question.

It was Assistant Principal Al Plotkin who one day (again in my first year of teaching) showed up at my ninth-grade math class with a note and a student named Jacque Dawes. I guess Freyer did not think that Jacque would make his way to my classroom without an escort.

Before leaving me and Jacque, Al looked at me and raised his eyebrows as if to say, "Good luck, sucker." Al then looked at Jacque, gave him a different stare which said, "Don't screw up, Jacque. This is your last chance."

Plotkin was quite a character. His face wore the years of a lot of stress. It seemed that he knew all 1,500 students in the school either by name or by reputation. He reminded me of the actor Jerry Olbach from *Law and Order*. He even had that same no-nonsense demeanor.

Every day during lunch, Al played bridge with a group of instructors, and his patience with me allowed me to eventually learn the game and join in. He liked and respected me, but for some reason, he loved to call me "Rookie." Which, in itself, is not so bad except for the fact that he called me "Rookie" for the next ten years. Ha!

Al was aware of the multitude of problems that Jacque presented. Everyone in the school, students and teachers alike, knew about Jacque Dawes. His reputation of being incorrigible preceded his transfer into too many classes. Most teachers knew that Jacque was a walking time bomb, ready to explode at any given moment.

Jacque, at 5'11", looked too old to be a ninth grader. He was, in fact, almost seventeen and had a scarred face. It was obvious to me that he had been left back (repeated a grade) several times during his rise (and fall) through the educational system. There were rumors that Jacque (who was born in Puerto Rico) was attacked by four gang members while riding home on his bike one day. They were trying to steal his bike. Big mistake for the gang members. Though Jacque was left with scars from the fight, rumor had it that he put all four gang members in the hospital.

Because of the quantity of students being transferred to my classes, I developed a private pep talk that I would give them before they walked into that first class with me. I always tried to have a brief conversation with my transferees outside the classroom while my classroom door was closed.

So, when Jacque ignored me and started to walk into my ninth-grade math classroom, I stopped him by physically blocking the entrance to the room. I told him that I would like to talk to him first. He stood directly in front of me with his head down and showed no interest in what I wanted to say. The first thing I said was, "Listen, we both know why you were transferred to my class. Let's make a deal. I don't care what you did in your previous classes or anything else from your past. You are going to start my class with a clean slate. In turn, I want you to pretend that I am the world's greatest teacher. Jacque, I am not your best friend, but I will be there for you if you ever need help, and I am not just talking about math. I am talking about your life."

He was still looking down. I continued and said, "Let's make one more deal. When you talk to me, I promise to look you in the eye and listen to every word you say. I would like you to do the same thing for me." He immediately looked up and stared at me eye to eye.

This was the first time I notice just how scary Jacque looked. His features reminded me of one of the juvenile delinquents from the movie *Blackboard Jungle* or a gang member from movie *West Side Story*. He just had that expression that said, "Don't mess with me or I will cut up your face."

He then looked at me and said, "We're cool, Teach, as long as you don't touch me."

Not knowing what to say and realizing that he was trying to take some control, I told him that he really wasn't really my type. I couldn't believe it, but he surprisingly broke out into a grin. Jacque, by reputation, had a problem with touching. If anyone touched him, it often led to a fight. He also, obviously, had a problem with authority.

He slowly walked into class, took an available seat, and didn't say a word the rest of that class session. He just sat there staring into space.

That afternoon, Plotkin came to see me and told me that I was Jacque's last hope. He said that Jacque was surprisingly quiet but just got into too many fights. Plotkin went on to tell me that I would have to keep Jacque out of trouble, or he was gone. He meant gone from school as in "expelled." Jacque, who rarely came to school, wasn't your basic bully. He didn't try to intimidate students or teachers. He didn't have to. He could intimidate people just by staring at them.

The next day, Jacque showed up to class. I only mention this because he had a track record of frequent absences. But again, he just sat there. No notebook, no nothing. After class, I called him aside. I asked him why he didn't have a notebook. He said, "What for?" Which is simultaneously both comical and sad.

I said, "Jacque, it looks kind of bad for me that you are the only one that isn't doing the classwork."

He looked me in the eye and said, "Okay, Teach, get me a notebook. See you tomorrow."

Well, I got him the notebook. The next day, he did take notes— or at least pretended to. The day after that, not only did he show up again, but he went totally out of character and asked a question in class. When he spoke, you could hear a pin drop. There was total silence in the room. The students and I were in disbelief.

The next day, I came up with a brilliant idea. As he was about to leave at the end of class, I went up to him and asked him to be my class assistant. I told him that I needed someone to pass out worksheets, collect homework, etc. "No problem, Teach. Whatever you need Teach."

I continued, "Oh, Jacque, could you do me one more favor?" He shrugged his shoulders, waiting for my request. I asked him, "It would be really cool if you called me 'Mr. Rand' and not Teach."

He stared at my eyes and said, "You got it, *Teach*!" And then he smiled and said, "Just kidding, Mr. Rand." That was quite a victory for me.

Asking Jacque to be my assistant helped create a bond between him and I, and it also kept the other students in line. Considering who was collecting the homework, they were fearful of not doing their assignment. Smart move, huh? Surviving as a rookie teacher in a New York City junior high school was contingent on making "smart" moves like that.

Jacque continued to improve as a person and as a student. For the next two weeks, he arrived every day in my class. This must have been a record for him. On the day of the following incident, I, unfortunately, was absent from school because I was sick with the flu.

Just as a side note, most teachers hate to be absent. I rarely got sick. I clearly remember wishing I could go to school that day because I was worried about my students, especially Jacque, but I just couldn't make it out of bed. In twenty-eight years of teaching at the community college, I was absent only six days. The timing of my illness could not have been worse because there was a school assembly. A teacher who was at the assembly did not know that Jacque was my classroom assistant and he got on Jacque's case for standing up and directing my students to their proper seats.

The story, relayed to me by Al Plotkin, was that Jacque was trying to keep my students quiet and in their correct seats. The teacher who was confronting Jacque did not appreciate a student taking that kind of control. One thing led to another, and the teacher and Jacque got into a verbal argument. The teacher, exerting his authority, pushed Jacque on the shoulder, trying to get him to sit down. Big mistake. Jacque got up, punched the teacher in the face, and broke his jaw.

There was nothing I could do.

They had to immediately expel Jacque from the school. The next day, I was still at home with the flu when I got a phone call from Al Plotkin. He told me about the incident. Knowing how much progress that Jacque had been making in my class, he said that he wished there was something that he could do. Al said that the best he could do was to try to convince the teacher not to press charges against Jacque.

After we hung up, I cried. I was becoming extremely fond of Jacque and saw that he had a lot of potential. I also felt responsible for the incident. I was just beginning to reach him. If only I had gone to school that day, none of it would have happened.

About two weeks later, I was walking to my car after school when Jacque approached me out of nowhere. Not sure what to expect, I just waited.

He came right up to me and said, "Sorry, Mr. Rand."

I looked at him and said, "No, Jacque, it was my fault. If I had been there, none of this would have happened."

He stared at me for a moment and said, with a tear in his eye, "No, Mr. Rand, it was my fault." He then said, "Thank you. You're the only teacher who ever showed that they cared about me." Then he walked away.

After about two steps, he turned around, came up to me, and gave me a hug. More tears, and this time it came from both of us. This young man, whose first words to me was a warning not to touch him, just gave me hug. The drive home was very difficult. This was an equally painful story to write about.

I later found out that Jacque never went to high school. The good news is that he became a member of the "Guardian Angels," which was kind of a neighborhood watch group whose mission was to keep local kids on the street safe from gangs and drugs.

It is the hope of every teacher to make a profound difference in the life of their students. Not realizing it at the time, but I can look back and appreciate that in my first year of teaching, I have been rewarded with some life-changing moments, both for me and my students. It's my students who are now making a difference in my life.

The answer to the opening quote is Ken Rand (me). I have said these words as part of my closing remarks on the first day of every class I have taught for the last twenty years.

Chapter Eleven

Learning to Connect

Who said the following:

"The mediocre teacher tells. The good teacher explains. The superior teacher demonstrates. The great teacher inspires."

   a)   Jim Riley
   b)   Kelly Locke
   c)   Jim Butler
   d)   William Ward

The answer is at the end of this chapter.

Necessity is the mother of invention, so it wasn't long before I invented my first board game for the classroom (among many that were to come later in my career) called "Aftermath." It was basically a monopoly-style board game where students would roll dice and go around the board and land on "addition" (or some other operation). After landing on the space, they could choose between a $100- or $500- or even a $1000-question based upon their perceived level of proficiency.

After the success of "Aftermath," which I was able to adapt to any mathematics level, I then invented "Common Knowledge." This game was similar to the math game; however, in this game I used a combination of math, English, history, and science as spaces on the game board. I also had the same levels of $100, $500, and $1000 questions (see graphic below).

Without knowing it, I had invented "Trivial Pursuit" and "Jeopardy" before these games were thoughts in anyone else's head. I remember bringing my game to the Toy Fair in New York City, where I visited the showroom of every major and minor game manufacturer only to have them tell me that the general public was not ready for a game of general knowledge. *Hmm? What am I missing here?* I guess it seems that there marketing experts were not so expert.

The board illustrated below was handmade by me in 1968.

It was goodbye to lesson plans. Well not really. My supervisor at City University required them, but I hardly ever used them, especially for my algebra classes. I was, as were my students, having too much fun to use those uninspiring lesson plans.

I did have one overall plan. No, I had two plans. One was to make math fun and the other was to make it as simple as possible. This philosophy forced me to think outside the box. It is a strange phenomena that most of my creative thinking came to me while I was commuting to and from work. What is also true is that many of my colleagues have told me that they also have some of their best teaching ideas while they are driving to and from work. There is a major problem in coming up with a great teaching plan when you are driving a car. As I mentioned before, I tend to miss too many exits on the freeway.

I continued to play basketball with my students almost every day after school, which helped me to fit in. It also added to the Mr. Cool persona. On the weekends, I also took quite a few of my students (usually is groups of 15–20) to the movies or ice skating (yes, I asked them to get permission slips). Quite often, on the weekends, I would invite a smaller group of students to my parents' home in upstate New York. I asked them to help me clean up our lawn (and get paid) or work in our backyard and get a free delicious spaghetti meal from my mom.

I can still taste my Irish mom's spaghetti and meatballs. My mom was an incredible cook. My parents' home (graphic below) was a beautiful split-level house in the New York suburb of Dobbs Ferry, in Westchester County, with a population of 5,426. Though only a thirty-minute drive from my school in the Bronx, the tree-lined streets and middle-class neighborhood with beautiful new homes were worlds apart from the south Bronx.

I also brought my students on field trips to my alma mater, Fairleigh Dickenson University in Teaneck, New Jersey. I wanted to show them that a higher education was a reality and not some fantasy. I wanted to give them hope. I wanted to give them a dream for their future. Without dreams, there is no future, at least not one that leads to happiness and success.

My popularity and reputation among the students were growing every day. I was beginning to realize that bringing students to my parent's home and on those field trips would help instill some hope in my students. Perhaps one day, with hard work, they could achieve the things they wanted out of life.

There was still one problem. I still didn't know how to teach. I was a good entertainer and I tried to make math fun, but I still did not have the skills needed to be a successful teacher.

There had to be a way to reach my students, even if it was "one student at a time," and I resolved myself to find a way to do it. During my first year of teaching, I was Mr. Nice Guy, Mr. Cool. However, I wrongly perceived that by being my students' friend, they would respect me and learn from me. This became only too apparent when my algebra students failed their final exam.

The answer to the extra-credit question is William Ward.

Chapter Twelve
Learning by Failing

Extra credit: Who said?

"There is no failure. Only feedback."

    a)   David Eary
    b)   Robert Allen
    c)   Tim Wallace
    d)   James Rand

The answer is at the end of this chapter.

I am still in my first year of teaching, and in spite of my success with my general math students, I know for a fact that I still did not know how to teach. I know this because of the testing results of my ninth-grade algebra students on their final exam at the end of the year.

I had two ninth-grade algebra classes. Both classes had about 35–40 students each. It was a pleasure to teach these students because they were more mature than my seventh and eighth grade students. For a math teacher, algebra is a pretty straightforward course to teach. It is very sequential in that each chapter's concepts were built upon those learned in previous chapters. I thought I knew what I was doing, but I was wrongly confident that my students were learning.

For all New York State high school courses, such as algebra, biology, history, etc., there was a final exam that was developed by a group in Albany, New York, called the Board of Regents. Each year, this Board created final exams for students in these classes, and they all took the exact same test on the exact same date and exact same time as any other New York State student taking the same course. It's what we now call a "universal" final exam.

Every year, the Board of Regents published a review book of the ten previous years' final exams. This review book was designed to be used as a study guide, and most teachers used these books to help prepare their students for the Regents final exam. Using this review book, I did my best to prepare my ninth-grade algebra students for this Regents final, which was given in June. After the test, I found myself looking forward to the graded results. I would soon learn that "My best was not good enough."

I cannot describe my sickening feeling when I received my students' scores and saw that only two of my seventy-plus students passed that exam. *Wow! Wow! Wow!* Do the math. Sixty-eight of my algebra students failed the exam.

It was the end of the school year, and I should have been looking forward to summer vacation, but I cried during the entire drive home. I guess you are beginning to figure out that I wear my emotions on my sleeve (and my face).

At first, I was angry at my students for not studying enough; however, I soon realized that it was not my students who failed me, but it was me who had failed my students. The realization that I did not know how to teach a regimented math course that was so mathematically simple for me was overwhelmingly depressing.

When I arrived home, I was almost too embarrassed to tell my dad, but he could read my face and knew that something was wrong. I told him about my failure. As always, he had great words of wisdom. He looked me in the eye and said, "You have two choices, son. Either you find a different profession, or you decide to learn how to teach." He paused but went on to say, "My gut tells me that because of your success with your other classes, you are going to be a gifted teacher, but it's your choice."

It was at that very moment that I chose to be the best teacher that I could be. I made an instant decision that whenever possible, I would visit the classes of every great teacher in the school. And I would make it a goal to go to every local and regional workshop on teaching mathematics. This failure was something that I would not allow myself to experience ever again.

It did not take long for me to realize that I had made a terrible mistake by thinking that being my students' best friend was the way to educational success. This may have worked with my lower level students, but it was not a disciplined approach to teaching. I needed to stop living and teaching in a cocoon and begin to reach out to every possible resource.

The failure that I experienced with my first-year algebra students as previously described, among other things, was the driving force in my life as a teacher. I don't know if you can imagine how I felt. It was overwhelming. I loved my students and many of them loved me. Some of them were beginning to be part of my family. But I had to learn how to teach.

During my second year of teaching, even while I was working in the special program, I made it a point to visit the classes of every good teacher in our junior high school. I needed to see, firsthand, what good teaching was all about. And that's exactly what I did.

All these teachers had one thing in common. They all had total command of their students, and they all had incredible classroom management skills. All their students were listening and taking notes, asking questions, etc. But how were these instructors able to do this?

There was a gifted math teacher in the junior high school named Bill Weiss. I was truly amazed when I observed his class. Every student was taking notes. Every student was paying attention. His students were freely asking questions and volunteering to show off their work on the blackboard. I could clearly see that he had set routines which helped him maintain order and the learning environment in his classes. It was obvious that these established routines helped him have total control of his classroom and dynamics. It was equally obvious that he also had the complete respect of his students. This was true of all five of his classes. To this day, I don't think he was ever aware of how much I learned from him. Thank you, Bill.

I also visited the classes of many other teachers. Though these instructors were all very popular among their students, it was easy to see that they were teachers first and friends second. They demanded respect, not by asking for it but by expecting it and by not tolerating or allowing anything less. They all had set routines in the classroom, and their students knew these routines, and they were well aware that they were expected to follow through on them.

I also decided to go to as many city and statewide math conferences as possible. I wanted to learn the tricks of my trade. I wanted to learn how to make math both fun and interesting. I wanted to learn about creative teaching methods, and these conferences showcased some of the best instructors in the educational system. In essence, I wanted to learn how to teach.

I soon went out and bought about some new suits (buy-one-get-and-one-free sounded good to me). Again, I wanted to look older and I wanted to look professional. Kind of what I thought a teacher should look like. The suits turned out to be a costly decision for me because I would constantly get chalk dust all over them, and I remember now that I must have had the world's largest dry-cleaning bill. New suits may have helped me looked professional, but they did not help make me a professional teacher.

The answer is Robert Allen.

Chapter Thirteen
"Your Best Is Not Good Enough"

Extra credit: Who said?

"Your best is not good enough" hint: movie

- a) Jaime Escalante
- b) Laurence Fishburne
- c) Richard Dreyfus
- d) Sidney Poitier

The answer is at the end of this chapter.

There are, of course, other things that inspired and motivated me. Some of them were movies about great teachers and great teaching. The movie *To Sir with Love* with Sidney Poitier was a big hit in 1967, and I personally found it to be very inspiring. For some reason, my students saw a little of Sidney Poitier in me and often called me "Sir." That was quite a compliment. It was much better than having them call me "Teach."

There are many other movies that continued to inspire me, among them are *Higher Learning, Dead Poets Society, Stand and Deliver*, and *Mr. Holland's Opus*, to name a few.

A few words about *Mr. Holland's Opus*. This movie is meaningful to me in so many ways, but there is a special line in this movie, which is repeated twice, and this line makes me wonder if it had a similar effect with other teachers. It's my guess that most of you who saw this movie probably do not even remember the line.

There are two scenes in the movie when the line "Your best is not good enough" is spoken. One is where Mr. Holland, a popular music teacher, played by Richard Dreyfus, gets frustrated when he is trying to reach his eighteen-year-old deaf son who continually rebels against him. In this scene, out of his frustration, Mr. Holland turns and says to his wife, "I just don't know how to reach him, I am doing the best I can," and her brilliant response is, "I guess your best is just not good enough." He walked away from his wife with a look of total frustration and puzzlement.

Okay, okay, good line, and it was true. There's more.

Later in the movie, Mr. Holland finds out that the school board is about to stop the funding for his music program. The board holds a budget meeting, and he decides to show up and fight for his program. At the board meeting, his passion takes over while he is trying to persuade the board to keep the program. The president of the school board, who also happens to be his former student, says to him, "Don't you think we want to save this program? There are no funds. We are doing the best we can."

Take a wild guess what Mr. Holland says to them. He, of course, says, "Then, your best is not good enough."

And that's when it hit me. As a teacher, I didn't ever want my best to be good enough. In my first year of teaching, I also thought that I was "doing the best I can," but it was obvious to me that this wasn't true. Especially after so many of my algebra students failed their final exam.

Even as a person, I didn't ever want my best to be good enough. I wanted to always find new ways, not only to inspire and motivate my students, but also teach them and myself how to be a better person. I wanted to keep looking for new ways to make math easier to learn.

It made sense to me that once your best "was" good enough, then there was no reason to continue and grow professionally. Basically, to me, once you became complacent and felt you reached the best of what you can do, you would then lose the most important reason to go on living both mentally and emotionally. This reason is the adventure of life. Continuing to grow and get better, to me, is an important component of what life was all about.

So, what do I say when one of my students comes to me after failing a test and say, "Mr. Rand, I am doing the best I can, I just can't get this. I studied for five hours for this test, and I did the practice test three times. I don't know what else I could have done." I have heard that frustrated plea too many times.

The first thing I do is to validate their effort. I tell them that I believe that they studied and tried their best. Next, I try to make sure I help them. I do whatever it takes and as long as it takes. I then ask them, "Do you ever try and study with a group?" to which most of them say, "I rather work alone" to which I say, "How has that been working out for you?" For most of them, this question allows a light bulb to go off in their head. And then I tell them the importance of that line from Mr. Holland's Opus.

The point I am trying to make is that sometimes, no matter how hard we "think" we are trying, our best is not always good enough, and we need to try harder. We need to explore other options. Options that we may not always feel comfortable with. There are times, as teachers, students, parents, and friends, when we need to go out of our comfort zone if we really hope to affect change both in ourselves and in others.

One afternoon, and this was still early in my career at this junior high school, I was having a short conference with my math supervisor (Mitzi DeLise) in her office and I happened to notice an attractive pamphlet on her desk. It was a catalog from a math education company called Creative Publications.

When our short conference was over, I asked my supervisor if I could borrow this catalog, she, of course, said yes. This became a life-changing moment in terms of my growth as a teacher. In that catalog were numerous games and workbooks and manipulatives designed to make math easier and make it fun.

A few days later, I asked my supervisor if there were any funds available for me to purchase some of the games, posters, etc. from the catalog. She gave me the hairy eyeball, relented, and told me that she could spare about $200 from the department budget. I matched that $200 with my own $200 and went shopping crazy. I bought as many games, posters, activity books, etc. that I could afford. It was inspiring to know that other teachers were creating products to help make math easy and fun. Little did I know that years later, I would eventually work for Creative Publications and go on to write some of their activity books (*Handy Math*) and invent games that were to be sold in Macy's, Sears, Kay Bee Toy and Hobby, etc.

Something magical happened in my third year of teaching. I was slowly becoming the type of teacher that I hoped to be. My lesson plans got better, my presentations improved, my confidence was sky high, and my students responded in a way that made driving home a pleasant trip. Good thing because I didn't need to lose any more hair.

I also got creative. After that, everything else was easy (or easier). I continued to use monopoly to teach math, I invented more of my own math games, and I went back to using lesson plans, and I got respect. Most importantly, my students, even in algebra, started to do extremely well.

It was in this year that I developed an opening-day speech. In this speech, I let my students know, among other things, that though I was available as a friend, I was going to be their teacher first and a friend second. I still interacted with my students after school and on weekends, but they all knew that Mr. Rand was committed to be their teacher. It was also during that third year that my reputation as a good teacher grew not only among the students but also among the faculty and administration.

I need to slow down and not get to far ahead of myself. In my second year of teaching, I was assigned to a special program. Michael (from Chapter One) who was placed in this program soon became the recipient of a classroom miracle. If I was not there to witness this event, I would not have believed it.

The answer is Richard Dreyfuss.

Chapter Fourteen
The Program: "Why?"

Extra credit: Who said?

"One child, one teacher, one book, one pen can change the world."

a) Mahatma Gandhi
b) Martin Luther King
c) Malala Yousafzai
d) Robert Kennedy

The answer is at the end of this chapter.

In order to truly convey to you what was soon to happen to Michael, I need to explain and describe the special program that Michael and I were both assigned to during my second year of teaching.

In the summer after my first year of teaching, I received a surprise phone call from the school administrative assistant. I was asked by her to drive down to the school and meet with the school principal. My thoughts were simply, *Hmmm?*

I asked her why, but she was somewhat evasive. All she said was, "Dr. Freyer has something important to discuss with you." I had absolutely no idea what to expect. My next thoughts were, *Oh. Oh! What did I do now?* It wasn't uncommon for me to be called to the principal's office. *This is summertime, I am supposed to be on vacation.*

I'm a born worrier. I always think of the worst-case scenario. Convinced that I did something wrong, I drove down to the Bronx, rehearsing a speech that will hopefully keep me from being fired. I don't like to beg, but I am ready to do so. *Relax and take a deep breath.*

When I arrived at Freyer's office, I was greeted by two veteran master teachers, Tony Falbo and Frank Hurst. It was common knowledge among the teaching staff that these were two of the best teachers the school had to offer. Now I'm thinking, *Why am I here in the middle of summer in the principal's office with two of the best teachers in the school? Have they been selected to tell me the bad news?* I would soon find out.

Also attending the meeting was Robert Treat, a psychologist from the Soundview Mental Health Clinic in the Bronx. *Maybe he will find out that I am too emotionally immature to be a teacher?*

Dr. Freyer got right to the point and told the three of us that he wanted to create three new classes, one class for each of the three grades (seventh, eighth, and ninth). Each class would have fifteen to twenty of the most "emotionally disturbed" male students from that grade. Ah, I knew that "emotionally disturbed" was the reason for me being there. Basically, what Freyer really meant was "the worst kids in the school." Now I'm thinking, *Maybe getting fired is a better option?*

Freyer told us the reasons for these new classes, but this wasn't really necessary. Everyone who taught in this school knew that the overall tone of the school was becoming unmanageable. Too many students in the halls during class. Way too many disruptions in the classrooms. Too many fights. If you have ever watched a movie about inner-city schools, then you know what I am talking about. This daily insanity made teaching a difficult job even for the veteran instructors. There were times when I would come to the school in the morning half expecting a student to have stolen the roof off the top of the building. It was that insane.

The psychologist, Bob Treat, described a special type of program for these new classes. To keep it simple, he would name our new project "The Program." According to Dr. Treat, what made The Program different was the philosophy where the students would be responsible for each other's discipline problems. It was sort of group therapy using peer pressure.

I'm now thinking, *Slowww down! You're telling us that we are going to be the teachers for the sixty worst students in the school and that we are not supposed to discipline them? Not going to work. Nope. No way, Jose. You must be on drugs!*

My role in our program was to teach mathematics to all three grade levels. The eighth-grade class of these "special" students was also going to be my homeroom class where we would meet early in the morning (8:00–8:30) and take attendance. I would also be asked, as were the two other instructors, to supervise the daily one-hour meeting of my homeroom students which took place at the end of the school day between 2:00 and 3:00.

Mr. Treat went on to tell us how lucky we were to be in The Program, a program that could very well change the lives of our students. I didn't feel so lucky. Apprehensive is the only polite word I can think of. For the record, Freyer did not ask us if we would volunteer for this assignment. He was not looking for volunteers. We had no choice.

Before our meeting ended, Bob Treat handed us the one-hundred-page program manual. He told us to be sure to read it before the start of school, which was now just a few weeks away. After the meeting, Falbo, Hurth, and I just kind of looked at each other with confused faces. Though not a word was spoken between us, I could see that they too were stunned.

As I am driving back home to Dobbs Ferry, New York, which is in Westchester County and about a thirty-minute drive from the Bronx, I am thinking again, *Why me?*, and I'm beginning to wonder about the implications of separating the sixty worst students in the school from the mainstream student population. By the way, for teachers, "thinking and driving" is an occupational hazard. I cannot tell you how many exits I have missed on the freeway because I was having a moment of creative genius (or worrying about getting fired).

Over the next two weeks, I read the manual, and after reading it, I was both amazed and yet still skeptical. Amazed because stories in the manual showed how through peer pressure, students could help each other change their poor behavior patterns. I was also very skeptical because the whole idea of students handling their own behavior problems sounded kind of risky. Especially for junior high school students who were guided by hormones which added to their lack of maturity.

The day before school started, I was given the roster of the names of my eighth grade students. I was delighted to see that about half of my new homeroom students were among those students who had been transferred to my class that prior year.

I was more than delighted. I knew a few of them quite well. I was even invited over to some of their homes to meet their families and have dinner. I had already developed that very important rapport with many of them, and now I'm beginning to feel a little more hopeful and comfortable. I'm even allowing myself to fantasize about the possibility at having a shot at changing the lives of these students.

The question is, will the program work?

The answer to the quotation is Malala Yousafzai.

Chapter Fifteen
The Program Begins

Who said the following:

"I teach because I love it. I cannot give it up."

- a) Jaime Escalante
- b) Eleanor Roosevelt
- c) Ken Rand (me)
- d) Johnny Perez

The answer is at the end of this chapter.

It's now the first day of class in September of 1968. I arrived early and rearranged the desks of my second-floor classroom (room 234) into a circle. This novel seating arrangement would make the upcoming discussion more workable.

As my nineteen program students walked into my room, I greeted them at the door. "How ya doin', Earl?" "Eddie, how was your summer?" "Michael, it's nice to see you again." I then directed them to sit in one of the chairs in the circle. In my mind, I'm trying to make believe that this is a normal classroom with normal students. This seating arrangement must have been strange to them because I remember most of my them giving me weird looks. Maybe it's not so normal after all.

Before everyone was seated and before I could say a word, one of my students said, with a very large question mark, "Why are we in this class?"

Someone else answered him, "It's because we're all stupid."

Another said, "You're stupid. Ha! I'm just plain crazy." They all started to laugh. Except for me.

What a start! I hadn't said a single word, and I had already lost control of my class. My prior thought of *This is going to be easy* was quickly brought back to reality. Then another student, who knew me from last year, looked at me with concern and asked, "Mr. Rand, why are we really here?"

I'm not sure how or why my students suspected that this class was "different," but their questions and comments definitely indicated that they knew something was up. Being twenty-two and naively hopeful, I was kind of taken aback. I wasn't prepared for this disruptive beginning. I then, instinctively, did what I do best and decided to go with the flow. I answered him with a bright smile, "You, guys, don't know how lucky you are to be in this class." This is what Robert Treat, the psychologist, told us teachers, and I am very good at repeating someone else's inspiring comments.

A student said, "Why's that?"

I responded, still with that big smile on my face and with false confidence, "First of all, you have me as your teacher." This brought some smiles. A few students who liked me even applauded. I'm now thinking, perhaps prematurely, that I am beginning to get back some control of class.

Trying to turn their negative preconceptions into something more positive, I went on to tell them, "Secondly, you have a golden opportunity that no other students in the school are going have." Now they are all listening to every word I say. *I'm now back in control.*

Roberto asked, "What's that?"

"This class, as you thought, is different, but it's a good different. The major difference is that you are all going to be in charge of disciplining yourselves. It will not be up to me or the other teachers.

You will have the power and responsibility to discipline each other." Their puzzled looks soon turned into comments.

Fernando, "Can you repeat that?"

Eddie, "You're kiddin'?"

Clayton, "You gots to be crazy."

Steven, "Not going to work."

Earl, "No way."

Hmmm? My program students were echoing my own thoughts of a few weeks ago. Now I'm wondering, *How am I going to get them to buy into this concept?* Within seconds, I had an unplanned stroke of genius. I took out the program manual, opened it, and said, "I am going to prove to you that this can work. Just listen and trust me. Let me read to you what this is all about." Their very skeptical eyes were now focused on me.

I started to read them excerpts from the manual that showed how the students in the original New Jersey High School program were able to help each other through peer pressure.

Eddie, not believing any of it, said, "Are you really reading this or are you making it up?"

My students looked confused and were shaking their heads in disbelief. I then handed the Manual to Charlie, one of my former students from the seventh grade, and I asked him to read. I did this knowing that he was very bright and a good reader.

Charlie started to read. After about five minutes, I asked him to stop. I looked at my group and said, "So, what do you think? Are you willing to give it a try?" It was kind of a rhetorical question, and I did not expect a response, but one by one, each of the students raised their hands in agreement, some of them more reluctantly than others.

This was a bonding moment and a good time for a break. "Hey, it's almost time for lunch. Let's go eat, and when we come back, we can practice doing the routines from the manual."

As I mentioned, we were separated from the mainstream of students, and our program students were given their own lunch hour. Picture this, there are sixty (all three program classes) very hormonal and uncontrollable boys and three teachers, and we had the entire cafeteria to ourselves. The noise level from our sixty misbehaving students was deafening. Students were running all over the place, and a few of them even tried to leave the cafeteria. Falbo, Hurth, and I all glanced at each other and quickly blocked the exits. *You're in prison, and you're going to stay in prison.*

During this chaos, the three of us are constantly exchanging smirks and glances at each other. We all felt that we should try to get them in their seats, but we also knew that The Program guidelines said that we were supposed to let them take care of their own problems. This unacceptable lunchroom behavior turned out to be a good thing. It gave us something to work on when we later got back to our program classrooms.

As soon as lunch ended, we went back to our classrooms. After a bit of a struggle, I somehow managed to get my students back in their seats. When calm was restored, I scanned their faces and said, "Did you notice that none of the teachers, including me, tried to stop the disruptions during lunch? We were hoping that you would try to stop it."

One of my students said, "You know, Mr. Rand, if anyone of us tried to stop it, there would have been a fight."

I said, "Probably true, but there is rule in The Program that would have prevented any fighting."

David, "Rules, I hate rules."

Eddie, "Rules suck."

Michael, "There's always a rule."

Jose, "What's the rule? No leaving to go to the bathroom?"

There were a few laughs.

Juan, "Teach, I got to goes. Real bad."

More laughter.

Leaving class to go to the bathroom was an all too common request from junior high school students. They would use any excuse in the book to leave class, and they probably could have written that book. "Yo, Teach! I need to go to the bathroom, and I have a note from my doctor." Ha, I once read one of those notes.

"Dere, Teach. Please let my paysent, Juan, go to the bathroom whenever he wants. He has bad kidneees. Signed, Juan's docter."

I continued, "Actually, you are allowed to leave the room to go to the bathroom anytime you want as long as your classmates approve." The surprised looks on their faces were priceless. I then said, "Do you want to hear the rule or not?" Another rhetorical question, but this time there was no response.

"The one major rule is the 'no touch' rule, which basically means no fighting. Anyone caught fighting in The Program would be expelled from school."

There were shocked looks among all nineteen of my students. I continued, "This means you can feel safe that no one will start a fight with you. You can tell someone to get back in their seat, and they can't do a thing to you. No one in The Program is permitted to bring street behavior into the classroom. This is your last resort, guys. You can even politely ask a classmate to stop talking while I am teaching, and there will be no repercussions."

Juan said, "Did you say we would get a concussion?" The other boys laughed.

I went on, "I also have a second rule."

Clayton, "I knew it."

Fernando, "Soon the teach is going to tell us that there will be a third and fourth rule."

"No, just one more, and this rule is only for this class. My personal rule is that the word 'stupid' is forbidden in my classroom. Anyone who says this word in my class will lose their privilege to go to gym during our gym hour." Knowing that the gym hour would be their favorite part of any school day made this a very effective rule.

Someone then said, "You knows very well, Mr. Rand, that not fighting here in school could just lead to fights outside of school."

Here comes my big locker room speech. My response was, "All of you need to understand that you are now part of a team. You need to back each other up, both in school and out. This is what The Program is all about." I went on, "Tomorrow, when we go to lunch, your group, our team, is going to set an example for the other two classes. You're going to get your lunch and sit and eat and ignore any craziness that the other students are up to. You all know what pride is, don't you?"

Clayton said, "Yes, it's feeling good about yourself for doing something that others can't do."

I asked, "Can anyone use the word pride in a sentence?"

Eddie replied, "Yeh, like I take pride in coming up with excuses for missing school."

This was funny. I had to laugh. My students had a sense of humor.

"Imagine how all of you will feel tomorrow if you are the only students who can pull this off." The boys started to snicker, and I quickly realized my wrong choice of words.

Roberto, "Yeah, I know how we will feel, we will all look like a bunch of brownnosers."

Earl, "No, it will be cool. We can show those ninth graders that we are better than them."

Thank you, Earl. I love you.

Though there were a few looks of doubt, a collective smile of belief soon came across their faces.

For the next couple of hours, we practiced some of The Program routines by creating mock circumstances where they would use their own voices to stop someone else from acting out. Speaking of pride. While driving home from school that day, I'm feeling pretty good. As the comedian, Larry David, would say, I'm feeling, "Pretty, pretty good." And I only missed two exits.

The answer is Eleanor Roosevelt.

Chapter Sixteen

"Sugar Pie Honey Bunch"

Who said the following:

"A life is not important except in the impact it has on other lives."

    a)   John F. Kennedy
    b)   Madeline Albright
    c)   Martin Luther King
    d)   Jackie Robinson

The answer is at the end of this chapter.

The next day, three of my students were absent. This was disappointing because it was only the second day of school. After taking attendance, I asked the class. "What do you think we should do?"

Eddie said, "Are you trying to tell us something?"

Earl answered for me, "Don't you remember what Mr. Rand said yesterday, 'We are all here to help each other.'"

Hmm? Earl is beginning to understand The Program. What happened next borders on the incredible. Without a word spoken, they all looked at each other and grabbed their coats and started to leave the class. Coats in September? Yes, junior high school students wore their coats even when they were sleeping.

I'm confused. "Hey, where are you going?"

"We're going to get them out of bed and bring them to school." That was Earl speaking, and he had this great big grin on his face.

Now I'm thinking, *Holy shit. What have I done?* I'm also wondering, *Are we allowed to do this?*

Not knowing what to do or say, I again went with the flow and asked them if I could join them.

Fernando, "Don't trust us, huh?"

I laughed and said, "Not yet?"

Everyone smiled. We were beginning to become a team.

Well, they were able to get all three embarrassed students and bring them back to school. What was probably just an excuse for my students to leave school and not do any classwork became an early turning point in their newfound power.

Alberto, "Are we allowed to punish them?"

Me, "What do you mean?"

Steven, "We know we can't touch them, but can we take away some privileges?"

Me, "I'll tell you what. During the last hour of the day, we will have our afternoon meeting, and you can discuss then what you want the punishment to be. For now, we need to get down to work."

Juan, "Can we just go out and look for some more absent students?"

We all laughed.

Before lunch, I reminded my students about our pledge to have a quiet lunch hour even if students in the other two classes were acting out. It worked!

My students were fantastic. Falbo came up to me during lunch and said, "Are you giving them drugs? What did you do? Are you paying them to be quiet?"

I looked at him, smiled, and said, "Tony, everyone enjoys a little competition."

He shook his head, smiled in return, nodded, and he said, "Game on, Rand."

This is only the second day of The Program, and my students are already buying into it? I am also having a hard time believing it myself. As a reward, I took some liberty and brought my eighth-grade program students to the newly constructed piano/organ room, which had about twenty-four brand new piano/organs. I told them that as a reward for excellent behavior, I was going to try to teach them how to play the piano. I also told them that I might have a surprise for them for later in the week.

Oops, I almost forgot. In the afternoon meeting, my homeroom students evidently liked sitting in a circle. They used this arrangement to sit together and discuss their fellow classmate's behavior problems or sometimes even their academic problems.

According to the guidelines from The Program manual, I was instructed not to take part in the meeting. I knew however, this was only the second day of school and my students needed more practice and guidance. So, I decided to be a presence in the afternoon meeting until I felt secure enough that they were getting the hang of it.

At this afternoon meeting, for the three absent students, the rest of the boys found an effective way to dish out punishment. They decided that whoever was the focus of the afternoon meeting would have to be on their knees in the center of the circle of chairs while the rest of the students were sitting.

The three culprits who tried to skip school were told by the group to get on their knees. They, of course resisted, but the rest of the boys reminded the three that they were among those who raised their hands the day before and said that they were willing to give The Program a chance. The three amigos reluctantly obliged. It didn't take long for all of them to swear never to be absent again. The floor of the classroom was just too hard. No carpets. *Ouch!*

Went I arrived home, I told my dad about this new piano room and asked him to come to the school and play for us. Dad was a professional pianist who also taught private lessons for a living. He was a graduate from the Julliard School of Music in New York City and studied to be a classical pianist. I am proud to say that he was at the top of his class.

There wasn't much money in being a classical musician, so Dad went on to be a successful band leader and private music teacher. Because of this career (and his perfect pitch), my dad was well-versed in the contemporary music of my students.

That Friday, my dad came to school and was able to play any song my students requested. After playing for about forty-five minutes, one of the students shouted, "Papa Rand, can you play the Temptations?" My dad quickly obliged. I didn't even know that my dad knew these songs. The bell for dismissal rang, but my students called out, "One more, just one more."

I whispered in my dad's ear, "Can you play the Four Tops?"

Meanwhile, I didn't realize that a crowd of students had gathered outside the room. Again, without hesitation, my dad started to play one of their most popular songs, and within the first four rhythmic notes, everyone in the room stood up and started dancing and singing.

Sugar pie, honey bunch
You know that I love you
I can't help myself
I love you and nobody else
In and out my life
You come and you go
Leaving just your picture behind
And I kissed it a thousand times...

Four of my students formed a line and started to imitate the signature dance moves of the Four Tops. The class went wild with excitement. I also couldn't help myself and started moving to the beat. One of my students saw me "moving" and said, "Mr. Rand, dance with us."

I told him, "It's the 'Four Tops,' not the 'Five Tops.'"

That didn't work. They pulled me over, and I was soon dancing with them. At twenty-two, I am a much better dancer than I am teacher.

That large crowd of students outside the closed door was getting bigger, and they were dancing in the hallway, wishing that they could come in. There were a lot of students late for their next class. My dad's talents, of course, made me an instant hero with my students, but it got me in trouble (again) with Principal Freyer.

Later, when school was over, I was summoned to Freyer's office. This was not my first trip to his office. Walking to his office is like walking the green mile. I approached his office door with extreme caution and anxiety. I walked in. He motioned for me to sit down. I choose to stand.

Freyer, "You can't do that."

Me, "Do what?"

His ashtray of cigar butts went flying by my head.

Freyer, "Sit down."

I guess he wanted a stationary target. He closed his door. Now I'm thinking, *This is it. Now I'm really get fired.*

"You need to get permission to have a nonschool employee come into the school."

I told Freyer that it was my dad who played for my students. He then said, "I don't care if it was Liberace. Do you know the disturbance you caused?" That was a question he really did not want an answer to. "How did you get the key to that room anyway?"

I told him, "I asked the janitor. He didn't seem to object. Sorry, Dr. Freyer, I thought I did the right thing. Next time I'll make sure you know."

Freyer, shaking his head, gave me his infamous and all too predictable closing remark, "Get out of my office."

I lived to teach another day.

This entertainment from my dad inspired my students. They now wanted to learn how to play the piano. Though I was not gifted like my dad, I was fortunate enough to have inherited about 10 percent of his talent. This minimal amount of talent gave me enough skills to be able to teach them some simple songs. Teaching them music was also a great way to break up a rigorous day of classwork.

Twice a week, we went to the piano room where I would try to teach my "incorrigible" students some of the hottest songs they were listening to on the radio. I also chose some of the older songs like Marvin Gaye's "What's Going On" and Simon and Garfunkel's "Sounds of Silence." I purposely choose these songs because the lyrics had some deeper meanings.

My plan and hope were that these songs would prompt some classroom discussion. I even printed up copies of the lyrics to use as reading, writing, and social studies lessons. What was truly incredible was that it wasn't long before I was able to get them to listen to and enjoy classical music. Yes, classical music.

I clearly remember one day when Mr. Falbo poked his head into our room while my students were listening to Tchaikovsky's "1812 Overture." Falbo just looked at me cross-eyed and said, "Rand, you're crazy." This specific classical piece led to a great lesson in world history.

Playing music in the classroom became one of the many common practices I would use as teacher throughout my career. I would even play different songs depending on the occasion. For example, before giving the first test of the year, I would ask my students, "How are you feeling about this test? Raise your hands if you are nervous about it, maybe you're even a little shook up." Usually more than half the class would raise their hands.

I'd then say, "I think I know how you feel, and so does a very famous person." I would turn my back to my class, put up the collar on my shirt, put on my sunglasses, then turn around and press the play button on my very large portable radio cassette. In seconds, they would hear Elvis's "All Shook Up." I can't sing, but I lip-synch the words as if I was really singing.

> Well, my hands are shakin' and my knees are weak
> I can't seem to stand on my own two feet
> Thank you. Thank you very much.

Not wanting to waste a great moment, I would also imitate Elvis's dance moves. My students would laugh, relax, and calm down. It worked every time. This worked a lot better when I was in my twenties than when I was in my sixties, but I still tried. Ha!

The answer to the extra-credit question is Jackie Robinson.

Chapter Seventeen
Michael: Story No. 2

Extra credit: Who said?

"In learning you will teach, in teaching you will learn."

    a)   Elton John
    b)   Phil Collins
    c)   Diana Ross
    d)   Michael Jackson

The answer is at the end of this chapter.

I know I got carried away with describing The Program, but it's interesting, right? Plus, you needed this background to fully understand the impact that The Program had on my students and the way they were soon going to react to Michael.

This second story about Michael took place after we were already in The Program for a few months. At this stage in The Program, part of my role was to be a daily observer for the afternoon meeting which took place in the back of the room. While the students were conducting their meeting, I would sit at my desk about 25 feet away. Quite often, while observing the meeting, I would take notes and sometimes I would even tape-record their discussions.

What is important to note is that by this time, the students in my class had already begun to demonstrate a high degree of management for their meeting, including their newfound power of "peer pressure." There were some very valid reasons for a student not wanting to be the focus of the afternoon meeting. One is that the positive peer pressure worked. The other is that being on their knees for one hour was extremely painful.

At this point in The Program, Freyer made some significant changes to our teaching responsibilities. Each teacher now had their respective homeroom students for the entire day. That meant that I had to teach my homeroom students all the major subjects including English, science, math, and history (and, yes, piano). I asked Falbo and Hurth if we were legally allowed to teach these other courses. They both laughed and said, "Who cares?" Not having a teaching license for these other subjects did not seem to matter to Freyer either.

While I was giving a history test to my eighth-grade class, I noticed that Michael began to show signs of frustration, which he displayed by crumpling his test paper into a ball. He then spontaneously stood up from his seat and angrily threw the test paper on the floor.

Without me saying a word, as they were taught to do, a couple of his classmates told him to pick up the test. They immediately asked him to finish it. He refused. A couple of other students, not wanting to waste any more time, told Michael that today's meeting would be on him. To which Michael immediately walked out of the room. Not sure where he went, but he returned about an hour later.

Okay, so here is the picture. It's 2:00 PM. The school day's almost over. There are about eighteen of the toughest kids in school sitting on chairs in a circle in the back of the room waiting to help Michael. Michael is in the center of the circle on his knees on a very hard floor while I was sitting at my desk in the front of the room, not realizing that I'm about to witness a classroom miracle.

Michael immediately tried to be cute and said, "Can you guys hurry up? My knees are already starting to hurt." Wrong question to ask.

Roberto said, "Michael, we have a whole hour, we will stay longer if we have to."

Then someone else said, "Why did you tear up the test?" No answer from Michael.

Another student said, "Michael, why did you tear up the test?"

Again, no answer. There were some awkward moments of silence, almost as if the students were about to give up trying to help Michael.

After about a minute, another student looked directly at Michael and said, "Did you study for the test?"

Again, no answer, but the students and I could see that Michael was getting a little shook up.

Another minute went by, and Eddie said, "Michael, if you needed help for the test, we would have helped you."

And then, surprisingly, Michael started to cry. This kind of stunned the group, and it had the same effect on me. We did not know it then, but this was a breakthrough moment for The Program. Michael was the first but would not be the last student to cry during a program meeting. Tough guys didn't often like to show any sensitive emotions to their peers.

Again, there was silence. Finally, one of one his classmates said, "What's wrong, Michael?"

Another classmate said, "Hey Mike, we're here to help each other," and another said, "Michael, you can tell us."

Michael, already with tears rolling down from his eyes, started to cry even harder. He finally said, "You guys don't understand."

They all answered in unison, "Yes, we do, Michael, we're all in this class together."

At which Michael said, through his tears, "I can't read."

What was about to happen during that hour was, to me, one of the most amazing moments in my entire forty-seven-year teaching career. "Hollywood ending" does not seem to fit as a good description. This ending was real and not from some fabricated Hollywood script.

Eddie, "Michael, don't feel bad. I can only read on the fourth-grade level, my reading level is 4.6." (You need to remember that this was an eighth-grade class.)

Earl, "Mike, my reading level is 5.3."

Alberto, "Hey, Mikey, my reading level is 4.2."

With that, Michael said while he was crying (and now so much harder), "You, guys, really don't understand. I can't read at all. ***I can't even read the 'stop' sign on the street.***"

The boys in the group were again in total shock. The expression "oh my god" was not used at this time, but this would have been a great opportunity for it to get its start. They were so shocked that they didn't know what to do or say. They all turned their heads spontaneously and looked at me. They must have been wondering, like I was, *How does a student make it to the eighth grade without being able to read?*

The only answer I could think of was that no teacher wanted to be stuck with Michael for another year. Perhaps they simply passed him along to the next grade level. I'm not sure if my program students were really thinking this. It's probably more likely, however, they were just wondering, *Mr. Rand, what do we do now?*

At least a couple of very silent minutes went by when Michael asked, "Can I get up now?"

Then one of his classmates named Charles, brilliant Charles, not believing that Michael could not read and not wanting to let him off the hook, said, "Not yet."

Charles then went to the shelf at the back of the room, picked out a book, and opened to a page. He placed the book in front of Michael's face and said, "READ!"

Michael turned his head away from Charles and the book, and he said, "I just told you I can't read."

Charles was persistent. Michael, still on his knees, continued to turn his head away from the book every time Charles placed it in front of him.

Earl looked up at me and asked, "Mr. Rand, can we hold Michael's head to keep it from turning away?" He was afraid to break the "no touch" rule.

I told him, "Go ahead. You're not hurting him."

While Earl held Michael's head, Charles pointed to a word and asked Michael to read it. Michael had no choice but to try. Charles brilliantly pointed to the word "the" with the hope that Michael may be able to read the simplest of words.

With tears pouring out of his eyes, Michael opened his eyes and said, "I don't know where to start."

Eddie said, "What letter is that first letter?"

Michael looked at the word and said, "T."

Fernando said, "Can you say the 't' sound?"

Michael looked at Fernando then looked at the word and said "T, t, t, th."

"Keep going," Charles said.

Then Michael finally said, "The."

Here I was sitting at my desk 25 feet away, and I didn't really believe what I was witnessing. I was even getting emotional as I am writing this.

Then Alberto said, "Great, Mikey, you did it."

A wave of smiles went across the faces of the other boys in the circle. "Keep reading, we will all help you."

I must admit that I was so very close to tears as I watched my students (my crazy students) try to change the life of one of their classmates. Oh, at this point, the 3:00 PM bell rang for the dismissal of the school day. Not one of the boys left the room or left Michael. I'm not even sure they heard the dismissal bell at all.

The next word on the page was "house." Again Michael's classmates helped him sound out the word until he got it correct. One word at a time and one student at a time, they continued to help Michael sound out the rest of the words on that page.

Then Charlie closed the book and said to Michael, "From now on, you and I are going to study together."

Biennuto, in his broken English, said, "That make tree of us." And so on.

They then told Michael that he could get up and sit down. He was no longer crying. In fact, he had a slight smile on his face. Not me. My emotions were going wild, and I was trying super hard not to show them my feelings. To say that I was proud of my students is a gross understatement. Good thing they didn't even notice I was

KEN RAND

there. This was their magical moment, and they had managed to totally block out that they were in a classroom with a teacher.

All the boys, including Michael, slowly got their schoolbooks, left the classroom, and went home. To my pleasant surprise, one minute later, Michael came back into the room, went to the book-shelf on the back wall, grabbed the book he had been forced to read, and brought it home with him. As he was walking out the door, he looked at me with a smile on his face—that beautiful infectious smile of his—and said, "See you tomorrow, Mr. Rand. I hope you can give me a makeup test. I may need your help with some of the words."

What became obvious to me was that at one time in his life, Michael knew how to read. Apparently, some traumatic event must have affected him so much that it repressed whatever reading skills he may have had. What I found to be fascinating was that Michael's classmates, these so-called "worst kids in the school," were able to make a difference in his life in a way that no other teacher or coun-selor could.

Yes, it's true that it's my second year of teaching, and I don't know how to teach, but I do know how to "learn." On the drive home that day, I began to develop a new teaching philosophy. A philosophy that educators today would call a "holistic" approach to teaching. I knew it was my job to teach them math, but at that moment, I realized that I had to first teach my students how to learn. This meeting taught me that in order to reach them, I had to teach the "whole" student. I had to find ways to inspire them in much the same way that they had just inspired me.

There is some bad news and good news. The bad news is that the funding for this special program stopped in April of that school year. That meant that my program students had to be mainstreamed back into regular classes for the remainder of the year. The good news is that most of them became leaders in their new classes and, in fact, leaders in the school.

Later that year, teacher after teacher would come up to me and say, "What did you do to Earl?" "What came over Fernando?" "Eddie

Perry is a changed student." "I can't believe that Michael is staying in his seat."

I told them with conviction, "I had very little to do with it."

To a person, these teachers said that my program students took over all the discipline problems in their classes and that teaching in a New York City junior high school had never been so good.

The next year, Charles ran for student council president. And won.

The answer to the extra-credit question is Phil Collins.

Chapter Eighteen
He Has a Gun

Extra credit: Who said?

"I never teach my pupils, I only attempt to provide the conditions in which they can learn."

    a)   Albert Einstein
    b)   Johnny Perez
    c)   Jaime Escalante
    d)   Woodrow Wilson

The answer is at the end of this chapter.

There were times when it felt like the only sane and safe place in this junior high school was in my classroom. There were always students running in the halls, banging on classroom doors, pulling fire alarms, etc. And there was always a daily fight either in a classroom or in the hallways. None of this ever happened in my classroom, but I had no control over what happened in the hallways.

One day during the change of periods when I was walking to my next classroom, a former student ran up to me and frantically whispered, "Mr. Rand, he has a gun."

I was confused. I asked him, "Who has a gun?"

He pointed to this student walking in the hallways during the change of periods (who I did not know). Sure enough, this student was holding a small pistol in his right hand. The fact that this student was barely five feet tall probably gave me some false confidence. My instincts and stupidity quickly took over. I quietly walked past this student on the other side of the crowded hallway and made a sudden U-turn after I passed him so I would then be directly behind him. I quickened my pace until I was walking right next to him. Then I bent over, whispered in his ear, and simultaneously grabbed his hand and the gun with as much strength as I could. I said, "Let go of the gun or I will break your hand."

He really had no choice. He was in obvious pain from my grip. Luckily his finger was not on the trigger. He winced in pain, relaxed his grip on the gun. I took the pistol out of his hand, pushed him against the wall, and said, "Don't move." Within minutes, Mr. Plotkin, the assistant principal was on the scene and took the cowboy downstairs to the principal's office.

I never found out the student's intent with the gun, but later in the day while walking to my class, I saw Plotkin. He looked at me, smiled with approval, and gave me the thumbs up. At the end of the day, Plotkin went out of his way to find me. He came up to me and said, "Either you are very stupid or very brave," then he broke out into a grin and said, "I would have done the same thing." There was no doubt about that.

Gang War

There was another potentially violent incident that happened about a year later. It was early morning. I had just finished parking my car near the school. While I was walking toward the main doors of the school, right before the school was to open for the morning classes, I noticed about half of the student population filling up the front yard of the school. There seemed to be something happening right on the front steps of the school. I really couldn't see what was going on, but I could hear a lot of shouting and yelling.

When I got closer to the main doors, I noticed that two rival street gangs, with about twenty students on each side, were getting ready to start a gang war right there near the steps to the front of the school. These were not junior high school kids. I doubt if any of them even went to school.

Again, my instincts and stupidly took over. I ran up, stood directly in between the two rival gang leaders, thinking, *Where were the other teachers and the administrators? Are they hiding?* One of the gang leaders was on the top step holding a knife and the other was swinging a pair of martial arts nunchucks. Thank God, no guns.

I quickly made believe I was an authority figure and shouted with false conviction, "Put your weapons away. *Now!*" They both looked at me like I was crazy. I then said, "This is not the time and place. You're bringing your street problems onto school property. The cops are on their way. You all need to *leave now!*"

The gang leaders were still stunned by my bravado. So was I. *What am I doing?* I lied. No one called the cops. There were no cell phones in 1970.

"Look, your only chance not to get arrested is to leave. I have no problem with you. But you're here, causing trouble in front of my school." That was stretching it a little bit. I was making believe I was an administrator. "You need to take your grudges somewhere else."

Don't ask me how or why, but it worked. After my brazen speech, the two gang leaders looked at each other, nodded liked they would go to war somewhere else, and slowly walked off the front steps of the school. The leaders were still eyeing each other as they walked off the school property. I had no idea where they went or what happened after that. Finally, another teacher arrived, and I told her to call the cops.

But can you imagine the scene? I'm in front of the school, unarmed, breaking up a potential gang war with about four hundred student witnesses. Though I'm pretty sure that our students would have loved to see a brawl, they were also very proud of me.

While walking into the school, I was greeted by students and teachers slapping my shoulders with signs of congratulations. I'm sure they were saying nice things, but I was in too much shock to hear them. I later found out through some students that this whole event started as a quarrel between two of our own students. Supposedly, this male student disrespected his ex-girlfriend by calling her a "ho." Apparently, her brother was a gang member and his cousin was also a gang member. Of course, this was reason enough for a gang war.

I am no hero. I don't know what took over me to be so brazen and brave. Perhaps it was my protective instincts and loyalty to our students that took over my brain.

This was not the last time I would unfortunately follow my instincts.

The answer to the extra-credit question is Albert Einstein (a.k.a. Cousin Albert).

Chapter Nineteen
The Intruder

Extra credit: Who said?

"This is my domain, behave or I will tattoo your chromosomes."
(Hint: movie)

- a) Lawrence Fishburne
- b) Johnny Perez
- c) Jaime Escalante
- d) Sidney Poitier

The answer is at the end of this chapter.

New teachers, like me, were given one of three assignments during the school day. Either we had "hall" duty or the even worse "lunch" duty or the very relaxing "study hall" duty.

The study hall was located in the school library and was the best of the three assignments because our school librarian was not the typical stereotype librarian that you would see on TV. She sounded and looked more like a drill sergeant. She not only intimidated students but she also intimidated us younger teachers as well. It was such as easy assignment that only one teacher was needed to help the librarian. Very few of us new teachers were lucky enough to get this assignment because it was usually saved for the veteran teachers. Just one of their many perks.

Lunch duty, however, was a total nightmare. Try to imagine five hundred eighth graders asserting their hormones in a crowded lunchroom. I get claustrophobic just thinking about it. It was totally insane. As soon as we were able to calm down one fight, then another one would break out on the other side of the cafeteria. And, yes, this was a daily occurrence.

Hall duty was not a picnic either. I hated hall duty. Every teacher hated it because it inevitably led to daily confrontations especially with students who did not know you. There were approximately 1,500 students in the school, and a good reputation only went so far.

On any given day, there were students wandering the hallways and hiding in staircases, and they were usually up to no good. Some of them were hiding in the bathrooms sneaking a smoke or making out with their girlfriend, or in some cases doing both.

On this eventful day, while I was walking down the hall on the first floor, I noticed this rather large student. He was walking about 50 feet away from me, and I did not recognize him. At about 6'4" and at least 260 lbs., he did not look like a junior high school student. Too damn big and too old.

As he walked right past me, I suspiciously said, "Excuse me. Do you have a hall pass?" I said this already knowing that he didn't.

Without hesitation, his response was "Fuck you."

Hmm? Fuck me, huh? I started to walk toward him, and he walked away from me. He quickly began to pick up his pace. I found myself following him, also picking up my pace.

My direction took me right past the main office where I popped in my head and shouted, "Intruder in the halls. We have an intruder."

As I was getting closer to this very large young man, he suddenly took off running in the direction of the staircase leading toward the outside of the school.

Why did he run? One punch from him in and I would have been in "never, never" land. Again, my Superman instincts and stupidity took over. I gave chase. He wasn't too fast and was slowed down by his rather large bulk. I am not Hussein Bolt, but I did catch up to him. I was going full speed when I physically ran into him exactly as he went through the doors leading to the steps going down to the outside street. I was running so fast that I ran right on top him.

We both went flying down about eight steps leading to the outdoor exit. I luckily landed directly on top of him. However, neither of us were not really that lucky. His face was a bloody mess having directly hit the cement floor leading to outside of the school. The next thing I know was that I am being carried on a stretcher to the nurse's office. The pain in my shoulder was excruciating.

Lying in that nurses' office, I noticed that I could not move my left arm which was in a V shape around the back of my neck. My legs hurt too. About fifteen minutes later while I was still lying there in pain, I heard an adult male yelling. He wanted to get at the teacher who hurt his son (his 6'4", 260-lb. son). Not to mention the fact that his son was an intruder in our school.

Meanwhile, I was on the nurse's office bed, hidden behind one of those hospital-like movable curtains, and he could not see me. He could, however, hear me moaning. In a burst of anger, the kid's dad, also a giant of a man, pulled back the curtain.

When he looked at me with my arms and legs shaped like a pretzel, he went into shock and started to yell at his son. The next thing I see was him slapping his son in his face right in front me. Then he pulled his larger-than-life son by the ear and told him to apologize to me. Which he did. It was quite memorable.

I think, after this incident, I finally learned my limits about getting involved in potentially dangerous situations. To this day, I still cannot put on a jacket using my left arm first.

The good news was that there was never a fight in my classroom. My students liked and respected me too much to cause that much trouble. All this craziness always happened outside my room. My classroom was my sanctuary, in fact, that's exactly what I told my students. My classroom was to be their "safe" place, a place where they came for three reasons. One was to learn and the other was to have fun while they were learning and the third was that it would be a "safe" place for them to be.

As Jaime Escalante said in *Stand and Deliver*, "This is my domain, behave or I will tattoo your chromosomes."

Chapter Twenty

"Teach, what are you?"

Extra credit: Who said?

"The job of an educator is to teach students to see vitality in themselves."

    a)   Joseph Campbell
    b)   Eric Bostick
    c)   Johnny Perez
    d)   Chuck Beals

The answer is at the end of this chapter.

Always have a plan B.

Almost all teachers have some magical moments in class. Not all of them are life changing, but they are magical, nevertheless. You can't plan these moments. They just seem to happen. What we, as teachers, need to have, is the ability to be flexible and the ability to adapt. By doing this, we allow the impossible to be possible. We allow those magical moments to foster and to appear and to grow into something very special. So, having a plan B doesn't necessarily mean you need an actual plan (but that's okay too). What it really means is that you are ready for anything to go wrong (which has a bad habit of happening in a classroom).

Such a moment happened in one of my seventh-grade math classes. This was now my third year of teaching (1969). My growth and confidence as a teacher were beginning to be part of my teaching persona. I am kind of laughing to myself as I write this because my teaching persona was not any different than me simply being myself. And I am very good at that. But this time, what was different is that I had more knowledge and confidence.

In my short career as a teacher, I was beginning to feel that I not only did I have control over my classroom environment but that I was actually beginning to learn "how to teach."

One day, in my seventh-grade math class, while I was teaching my brilliant shortcut for long division, one of my students, Miquel, spontaneously called out and asked me "Teach, what are you?" I guess he wasn't too crazy about long division nor my brilliant shortcut.

Yes, I was as confused by his question then as you are now. It seemed to come out of nowhere. *What am I?*

As usual, I went with the flow and looked at him with a confused smile on my face and said, "I am white," at which the entire class, including Miquel, laughed.

He went on, "I know that. I mean what's your heritage."

Oh! I then told him. "Well, I am 1/2 Irish and 1/2 Russian. My mom is Irish Catholic, and my dad's family is Jewish and was from Russia and Poland." Then just for laughs and a challenge, I threw in a few other fractions. "By the way, I am also 1/8 black, 1/8 Puerto Rican, and 1/8 Asian." More laughter.

Lawrence, "I know you are part black. I've seen the way you dance."

I did a quick dance move, and my students laughed.

The problem was that the fractions and my skin tone did not add up, and everyone could see that I had no black, Asian, or Puerto Rican heritage. They also didn't seem to have a clue about the wrong fractions that I gave them (on purpose) until...a student named Umberto said, "Wait a minute. There's something wrong with the math? The picture doesn't look right."

"What picture?" I said.

Even though I knew what he was talking about, I was playing dumb. Umberto then said, "Can I come to the board and show you?"

To my astonishment and that of his classmates, he drew two circles. One divided in halves, the other divided in what was supposed look like eighths of a circle. The first circle that he drew showed me as being 1/2 Irish and 1/2 Russian. The second circle showed pieces of pie with 1/8 shaded for each of my other phony ancestries. Umberto looked at me then he looked at the class and smiled. "I am not stupid, Mr. Rand, you can't be 1 and 3/8 of anything."

Smart kid.

Time to switch topics. Guess what I taught that day? With Umberto's help, I taught my students how to draw some basic fractions, and the next day, I taught them how to add fractions, using these same types of pictures. As luck would have it, I had some supplies from Creative Publications that showed students how to create equivalent fractions. And the day after that, I taught how to add fractions without pictures, and the day after that I taught the almost impossible task of adding unlike fractions.

None of this had been in my lesson plans for that week. Being flexible made for a great week of lessons. These lessons on fractions also shows how weak my seventh grade students were with problems in the most basic of math skills. My guess is that a large percentage of the general population still has a difficult time with fractions.

Most of my students were able to perform this fraction math because of the multiplication fact drills that we practiced on a daily basis. I learned these extremely effective drills from my former seventh-grade math teacher, Mr. Shapell.

There are only a handful of teachers from my past that had a profound effect upon my life. One of them was Mr. Shapell. Not wanting to go into too much detail about him, I do think it is important for us to give credit to the great teachers we have had.

Mr. Shapell was a teaching genius. He realized that the key to success in mathematics was a complete and rapid knowledge of the basic skills of adding, subtracting, multiplying, and dividing. He knew, as seventh graders, that we were "supposed to know" how to do these basics skills way before we got to him as students. Yet he also knew that we had not yet reached the level of perfecting those basic facts that is needed for us to have the necessary confidence to tackle the more difficult math concepts. And he was soooo right.

His exciting and inspiring basic skills games turned us all into walking calculators. He turned us on to mathematics in a way where we no longer had normal student conversations on the way to his class. Our hallway conversations went like this, "Quick, what's seven times eight? You're too slow. Get faster. Nine times six, quick. Don't think about it."

Once we built up those skills and our confidence, the word problems that he would give us became that much easier. We did not have to worry about having the ability to "do the math." We were able to concentrate on the meaning of the words in the problems. He literally changed my math life forever. Try doing fifty basic multiplication problems in twenty-eight seconds and you will know what I mean.

Being able to adapt to unplanned obstacles is a very important skill to have as a teacher. These obstacles are not always as a result of student comments during an expertly planned lesson as you will soon see.

The answer is Joseph Campbell.

Chapter Twenty-One
The "Stare"

Extra credit: Who said?

"Share your knowledge. It is a way to achieve immortality."

a) Pope John XII
b) Mahatma Gandhi
c) Jawaharlal Nehru
d) Dalai Lama XIV

The answer is at the end of this chapter.

Teaching, perhaps more than any other profession, lends itself to these unexpected moments where the consequences can be embarrassing, frustrating, and even life changing as can be seen in the next two chapters.

An embarrassing moment: This incident happened in my fourth year of teaching. By now, I considered myself to be a seasoned professional. Ha! I've never felt like a seasoned professional.

I was teaching a math lesson to my seventh-grade class in junior high school when a guidance counselor knocked on my door. He signaled two fingers to me. indicating he needed two minutes of my time. I told my class that I would be right back. I went out in the hallway, closed the door, and started to speak to the counselor.

Well, the two-minute talk outside my classroom took around five minutes, and I could see and hear, through the door glass window, that my students were getting restless. In a few short minutes, the classroom noise got so loud that I got embarrassed and asked the counselor to wait while I took care of business.

I went back into the room, and it instantly got silent. I immediately put on my teacher "stare" and circulated the room with my eyes, daring anyone to say a word. The "teacher stare" is a very effective tool that I learned purely my accident.

I don't remember the exact incident, but I know that there was a time when my class was noisier than acceptable. I immediately stop teaching, and I silently looked at each and every student, made a powerful eye contact with a touch of anger in my eyes. I didn't say a word, not one word. That's how I developed the "stare."

I was obviously upset at my students. I felt they had embarrassed me in front of the counselor. To emphasize my anger and disappointment in my students, I then walked out of the room and slammed the door. Much harder than I intended. Oops.

Not only was the noise of the door closing extremely loud, but I completely shattered the glass window on the top half of the door. It broke into a thousand little pieces. At which the counselor looked at me, and a few seconds later, he started to laugh. I couldn't help it, I also started to laugh. When my students saw us laughing, they also let out a big roar.

I immediately went back into the room again and changed my smile to a very firm look of distain. I put on my teacher stare, and they all immediately got silent and stopped laughing. But then I couldn't help it, and I broke into a big smile and said "Okay, okay, my bad" and everyone laughed again.

I was able to do this simply because my students liked me, respected me, and trusted me. Laughing at yourself is sometimes a good thing to do.

Guess what happened next? That's right, I was called down to Freyer's office.

Freyer, "Sit down." Pause. "Were you born with the sole purpose of making life miserable for me?" (He did not want an answer).

Me: "I apologize, Dr. Freyer. It was a total accident."

Freyer: "Do you have anger management issues? You're lucky we have insurance. Now get out of my office."

I walked away with my tail between my legs.

The answer is Dalai Lama XIV.

Chapter Twenty-Two
Dorothy

Extra credit: Who said?

"One looks back with appreciation to the brilliant teachers, but with gratitude to those who touched our human feelings..."

    a)   Carl Jung
    b)   Sigmund Freud
    c)   B.F. Skinner
    d)   Jean Piaget

The answer is at the end of this chapter.

Dorothy Wilson was a student in my eighth-grade general math class. I was now in my fifth year of teaching at the JHS. Dorothy seemed to be the angriest student I ever had. She frequently, for some unknown reason, gave me the "evil" stare as if I said or had done something wrong. It was kind of my "stare" in reverse.

She looked older than my other eighth grade students, and she was big (about 5'7" and 200 lbs.). A very big girl. She had a soft black complexion, and she never smiled. She was frequently giving me these dirty looks, and she was also very intimidating to her classmates. She was never openly rude, but her behavior was a puzzlement.

Her demeanor never changed. I found myself wondering what I did or said wrong. On a number of occasions, I asked to speak to her after class, but she always made some excuse, saying she didn't have time to do so or that she didn't want to be late for her next class. I can clearly remember that she made me feel so uncomfortable that I always walked into class half expecting a confrontation with her.

I am not sure why I did what I did, but for some reason, right before the Christmas break, I went out and bought her a Christmas card which simply said, "Wishing you and your family a Merry Christmas and a Happy New Year" and signed it, "Your favorite teacher, Mr. Rand." This turned out to be a stroke of genius. As she walked out of class on the last day before vacation, I called her to my desk. She reluctantly strolled over, and I handed her the card. She looked at me like I was crazy.

The first day after the Christmas break, she came up to me after class and asked to speak to me. She asked me why I gave her the card, especially when she had been so mean to me. I told her that I believed that deep down inside, she was a good person and could be a great student if she tried. She said "Thank you" and started to cry. I asked her what was wrong. She went on to tell me that she had witnessed her dad and mom being shot and killed and that she hated the world and everyone in it. I was, of course, shocked, but everything started to make sense. What can I possibly say to someone who has been through this kind of trauma?

My instincts took over, and I asked her if her dad and mom would have wanted her to be a good person and student. She looked at me with more tears in her eyes and said, "Yes, they would."

After that day, Dorothy was a new person. She smiled at me every time she saw me, and this very bright young lady became an excellent student. One day after class, she came up to me and said, "Mr. Rand, I have a new nickname for you." Afraid to ask, she then said, "You're the Bomb." Her smile told me that I was a good "Bomb."

Again, we never know how much the things we say and do can affect the lives of our students. I am not sure that in today's politically correct climate, whether giving a card to a student (especially a female student) would be a good idea.

The answer is Carl Jung.

Chapter Twenty-Three
"I'm Spartacus"

Extra credit: Who said?

"In a completely rational society, the best of us would be teachers and the rest of us would have to settle for something less."

a)   Henry Ford
b)   Horace Elgin Dodge
c)   Lee Iacocca
d)   Louis Chevrolet

The answer is at the end of this chapter.

After about three months into my fifth year of teaching, my longtime frustration over our dilapidated and useless textbooks reached a peak. Not only that, but the reading level of the textbook was about eighth or ninth grade. This would have been okay if the students were reading at that level; however, most of my students were reading somewhere between the fourth- to fifth-grade level, thus making their textbook almost impossible for them to understand.

This, plus the fact that all our math textbooks were 10–20 years old, made them extinct. Not only were they outdated but many of them wore the damaged effects of their years in use. As a result of my frustration with the textbooks, I had a dramatic moment in my math class that caused another confrontation with Principal Freyer.

My teacher copy of the textbook was in bad shape, and it was falling apart at the seams. It was useless in too many ways. One day, out of frustration, I went over to the open window and dramatically threw my textbook out the window. Our classroom was on the second floor, and the book fell onto the roof of the first floor. I know, it was a stupid thing to do, but I was fed up.

One student, who just happened to be paying attention, raised his hand and asked "Teach...why did you do that?"

I told him that the math textbook was useless. "It's worn out and only good for giving homework assignments." And it really wasn't even good for that.

Incredibly, this same student looked at me, and he thought for a moment, got up, took his own badly conditioned textbook to the window, and he also threw it out the window. You can guess what happened next. It was an "I'm Spartacus" moment. Yes, within minutes, the entire class had thrown their math textbooks out the second floor window, and they took great pride in doing so. *Holy shit. What just happened?* I really wasn't trying to be a negative role model.

Well, if nothing else, it was a great bonding moment.

The next day, of course, I was called down to Freyer's office. I wasn't trying to break the record set by Frank McCourt (author of *Teacher Man*) for trips to the principal's office, but I just had this propensity for getting in trouble. The fact that I knew what was coming from Freyer did not take away the pain of walking those final steps into his office. Kind of like walking to the execution chamber.

Freyer started shouting even before I had both feet in his office, "Close the door."

Now I know I am in real trouble.

"Are you fuckin' crazy?" (He loved to curse.) "Is it true? Please, tell me it's a rumor?"

I calmly said, with my best poker face, "I'm not sure what you are talking about?"

He just stared at me and growled. I was getting ready to duck just in case a cigarette ashtray would go flying by my head. "Sit down!"

This is not looking good.

"Did you throw your textbook out the window and ask your students to do the same?"

I said, "Well, half of it is right. Yes. I threw my textbook out the window, but I never told my students to follow my lead."

He sat down and bent over his desk and kept shaking his head and was holding his head with both his hands on his desk, and all he said was "Why?"

I wanted to say "Why what?" but I didn't just in case he had another ashtray.

I finally got the courage to speak and told him that the textbooks we were using were useless and in terrible condition.

He said, "How are you going to teach without a textbook?"

I wasn't brave enough to tell him that I was going to use games that I would create or were already created to teach math, so I just told him that I would find a way to complete the curriculum without a book or I would write my own book if I had to (which I eventually did).

He just looked at me in bewilderment and gave me a piece of pink paper. *Oh, oh, this is it. I'm fired.* I was sure that this was my final notice. I asked him, "What's this?"

He said "Open it," which I did.

It turned out to be a bill for over $400 for the textbooks we destroyed. At that time, $400 was a lot of money. It's still a lot of money. I was only making about $200 a week. *Ouch!*

At least I still had my job, which I sorely needed to order to pay for those textbooks. In reality, he should have thanked me. The next year, the entire math department received new textbooks for all our classes. Yay!

My math teaching colleagues considered me to be a hero. Don Quixote strikes again. Freyer was a strange dude. The very things that I did to upset him turn out to be significant changes in the way the school operates.

The answer is Lee Iacocca.

Chapter Twenty-Four

California Dreamin'

Extra credit: Who said?

"What we want is to see the child in pursuit of knowledge, and not knowledge in pursuit of the child."

    a)   John Steinbeck
    b)   Henry Miller
    c)   George Bernard Shaw
    d)   Emily Dickenson

The answer is at the end of this chapter.

It is now 1976. I am in my tenth year of teaching. I am a pro. Not yet. There is still so much to learn. Perhaps I should say this now before I forget to write it in a future chapter. There is no doubt in my mind that I learned something new about my students and something new about the art of teaching every single time I walked into and out of a classroom. This was true for me in 1976 as it was true for me until I retired in 2015 after forty-seven years of teaching.

Over the past nine years, from 1967 to 1976, I have created and accumulated a number of games, worksheets, and fun activity pages for my students. One day, my department chair (Mitzi DeLise) asked me if I would like to give a Saturday workshop at the upcoming Bronx district-wide math conference. This was quite an honor, and it would be the first time I would ever present my materials to a large group of math educators.

Having years of practice, in public speaking, I was no longer nervous about the thought of giving a presentation and realized that I was not being judged. I was just there to show off my classroom creations. With well over one hundred teachers in an auditorium-type room, I was pleasantly surprised as to how many teachers would give up their Saturday afternoon to learn more about their craft.

I wasn't the only presenter there. A number of other teachers went before me and showed off a lot of their really interesting classroom gimmicks. I was impressed. I felt comfortable because I have spent the last ten years engaging and connecting with my students, and my presentation was something that I thought would have interest to my entire audience of math instructors. I was the last presenter because Mitzi wanted to save me for end of the day.

Among the games I presented were "Aftermath" and "Common Knowledge," as well as my fun activity worksheets for the game of monopoly. I had also created some innovative real-world worksheets that used topics, such as math in sports, math in traveling, and math in shopping. Mathematics is a lot more fun and more palatable when it pertains to everyday circumstances and common interests.

Let's just say, it went over very well. I had every teacher there playing games and interacting with each other. It appeared that they were learning and having fun at the same time. Just like my students. After my presentation, which took over an hour, a line of teachers formed in front of me. Most of the teachers were congratulatory and some were curious if they could buy my games and activities. Quite a compliment.

The last person on that line introduced herself as Maggie Holler. Maggie seemed to be about my age, and she had an air of confidence about herself. She said that she was here from California as an editor for Creative Publications and was on the East Coast looking for more materials for her company to publish. *Hmmm?* I told her that I was a big fan of her company's products and had used them quite frequently in my classroom. What a coincidence.

Maybe not. My cousin, Dr. Ken Harris, author of *Synchronicity: The Magic ⏤ The Mystery ⏤ The Meaning*, would not think it was a coincidence at all. He firmly believes that things happen for a reason. I think he's right. By the way, for even more of a coincidence, Cousin Ken, also taught with me for a few years at this same junior high school. After a couple of years of teaching, he decided to study to become a chiropractor, and like me, he has the gift of gab and is now a well-known and gifted inspirational speaker.

Maggie asked me if I ever thought of getting my materials published, and the truth was, except for my game "Common Knowledge," the answer was no. She went on to tell me about an upcoming convention of the NCTM (National Council of Teacher's of Mathematics), which would take place in Kentucky in late April. She also informed me that her company would be setting up a show table to display their products, and there would be dozens of other math teachers at the conference giving presentations on a wide variety of topics.

Maggie strongly suggested that I attend the conference and said that she would try to set up a meeting between myself and the company president, Mr. Dale Seymour. A few weeks later, Maggie called me. She told me that the meeting was a go and gave me the time and date. She also reminded me that it would be worth my while to stay a few days and take in as many other presentations as possible.

This was an enticing offer, but one major problem. I was living from paycheck to paycheck. The cost of this trip would set me back financially. In case you haven't heard, teachers do not make a lot of money. There would be expenses for the flight, the hotel, the food, parking, etc. However, the possibility that I would be able to get some of my materials published was equally enticing, so I took the leap of faith and decided to go.

When I arrived at the convention hall, I was overwhelmed. First of all, this was the first time I ever went to a national education convention. It was jam-packed with hundreds of educators. Secondly, there were about sixty educational vendors showing off their products designed for teachers to use in the classroom. I had a difficult time walking around because I brought about twenty of my own games and products for Dale Seymour to evaluate. I soon found the Creative Publications booth, and Maggie Holler volunteered for me to leave my products with them until my meeting with Mr. Seymour.

As I was walking around, I could have never imagined that there were so many companies dedicated to making products to help math teachers. The convention hall was bigger than a high school gymnasium and would take days for me to walk through the aisles to see each companies' table or booth.

My appointment with Dale Seymour was at 2:00 PM, and after taking a few hours to visit some of the exhibits in the convention hall, I made my way up to Mr. Seymour's hotel room. It was not a hotel room, it was a suite. This was another first for me. Wow, a suite. Very impressive. The living room was massive and decorated with beautiful chairs and couches. There was also a separate full-sized kitchen. I'm sure there were a few bedrooms, and it also had a huge balcony with a fantastic view of the Ohio River.

Maggie was there, and she introduced me to the company president, Dale Seymour. Dale was around fifty years old, had a California tan, he was rather slim and stood about 6'2" tall. He also had an air of intelligence and confidence about him. It was impossible to shake his hand because my hands were full of all the games and activities that I brought with me.

Dale asked me to have a seat. He got right down to business and said, "I heard you have some games and other products to show me. I'm ready."

I began to explain each of my products to him, which was somewhat difficult because we were constantly disrupted by people walking in and out of the suite. Each time someone would walk by us, Dale would politely introduce to me to them (not that I would ever remember their name). For me, these interruptions were a distraction. It's difficult to show off when you're constantly interrupted.

Well, as I said, I had about twenty different games, etc. to show him, and after I demonstrated each one, he would ask, with a stoic face, "What's next?" He eventually said "What's next?" at least twenty times. His facial expression did not change for any of my twenty short presentations. It just seemed to me that he had little or no interest in what I was showing him. After I was finished, he politely thanked me, told me that he was extremely busy, and hoped that I enjoyed the convention. That was it.

To say I was disappointed would be an understatement. *Was this a wasted trip?* To keep it from being that, I decided to read the available convention program, and I went to see as many teacher presentations as possible.

Good choice, Ken. I could not believe the amount of raw teaching talent that I observed in these presentations. It was extremely satisfying to see that so many other math teachers were creating and doing things in their classroom to make learning fun.

I went back to New York with mixed feelings. There was no doubt that Mr. Seymour was not impressed with anything I showed him; however, I did learn a lot from the other educators that gave their entertaining presentations. I was even eager to get back to my classroom and try out some of things I learned there on my students.

Just for example, one teacher told us about this gimmick he had where he told his students that if he made three mistakes during class, then they would have no homework. He went on to tell us that he often made one or two mistakes on purpose. After the second mistake, he had every student in the class on the edge of their seats, waiting for his third and fatal mistake. This gimmick became part of my opening-day announcement in my classes for the next thirty-seven years.

Two weeks later after the convention, while I'm home grading papers, the phone rang. The woman on the other end introduced herself as Jolene, the secretarial assistant to Dale Seymour. She asked if I was Ken Rand. I said "Yes."

Then she said, "Can you wait a minute, Mr. Seymour would like to talk to you."

Huh? What was this about?

DALE. Hello, Ken, how are you? How was the convention?

ME. I'm doing fine, Mr. Seymour. I had a great time.

DALE. Please, call me Dale. (*Pause*) I have a proposition for you. I was really impressed by your presentation to me, and I was even more impressed by you and your passion for teaching and making math fun and exciting.

Now I was really confused. This guy must be the world's best poker player. When I saw him in Kentucky, his face revealed little interest in me and in what I was showing to him. A very shocked me said, "I'm listening."

DALE. Instead of us (Creative Publications) publishing your materials and giving you a royalty, I am wondering if you would come to California and like to work for us?

What? There must be something wrong with our phone connection. I was in so much disbelief that I didn't answer him.

DALE. Are you still there?

ME. Dale, I am a little surprised that's all. I didn't go to see you with the hope of getting a job.

DALE. I know. But I think that this is a great opportunity for you.

At this point, I was confused, surprised, and a little in shock. I wasn't really sure what to say. But somehow, I think I found the right words.

ME. Mr. Seymour, Dale, I am a teacher. I love to teach. I love my students. I never thought about doing anything else.

DALE. Let me ask you a question. How many students to you teach each year?

ME. Maybe about three hundred or so.

DALE. You told me that you been teaching ten years, so that means that over the course of your career, you have probably taught about three thousand students.

ME. That sounds right.

DALE. Well, I am giving you the opportunity to reach over one hundred thousand students and thousands of teachers."

Now I was thinking, *Wow, wow, OMG. This is wild. What do I tell him? Somebody pinch me. One hundred thousand students? That's a lot.* This was an overwhelming thought.

DALE. This is a great place to work, and the Bay Area is a great place to live. My company is dedicated to reaching teachers and students of mathematics. We have a fantastic team of brilliant people working here to help me create new math products for the classroom.

He's a good salesman. He's making me think about it.

ME, *still in shock.* Dale, thank you for the offer, but is it okay for me to think about it for a few days?

DALE. Sure, take your time. You probably need to know that we will pay you $10,000 more per year than what you are making now, and we will also pay for your trip to move out here. We also have some great medical benefits too.

He really was a good salesman.

ME. That's good to know. Thank you, Mr. Seymour, I mean Dale. I will definitely call you in a few days.

DALE. Please do. Nice to talk to you, Ken.

I wasn't bullshitting him. Ten minutes ago, I never had a thought about leaving the classroom for a different job. Well, that's short of a half lie. I did, at one time, want to be a school principal. I would often fantasize that being a principal would allow me to hire the very best teachers and create an educational environment where learning was fun and exciting. I could even see myself, as a principal, standing on the front steps of the school, giving warm and friendly greetings to each of my students as they arrived.

At the time of this interview(?) with Dale Seymour, I was in the middle of pursuing a PhD in administrative education at New York University (NYU). I already completed thirty units and needed thirty more to finish my degree. Getting a PhD in educational administration would open up a lot of doors for me. However, the flip side was that leaving the classroom to be an administrator was somewhat of an uncomfortable feeling for me. The classroom was my domain. I came to life in the classroom. It's kind of difficult to explain.

Being an administrator presented an obstacle. Would I be able to teach and be a school principal at the same time? I never heard of a school principal who was also a teacher. In my fantasy, I made a commitment to becoming the first. I loved being in the classroom and found it emotionally difficult to let go of that.

This offer from Dale was so completely unexpected. Now I have to think. I have to weigh the pros and the cons. I remember that this is exactly what I did. I took out a piece of paper and drew a line down the middle, and the heading on the left side was "Pros" and on the right side I wrote "Cons." I'm laughing now because I remember that piece of paper had just as many thoughts on the left side as it had on the right side.

I am a New Yorker. I was born in New York and have lived my entire life there. Everyone that I knew, either as a friend or family, lived there. Wow, leaving my family. That was a tough one. However, living in California, hmm? Life is easier there, isn't it? Maybe I will live ten years longer if I move and live there?

During the time of this interview with Dale, I was married to my wife, Maria, who happened to be a former student of mine. I don't know if there was something in the air, but I know for a fact that at least five teachers in my school married former students.

Not sure if you remember the song by Ben E. King called "Spanish Harlem," but I believe that when you see beauty among the thorns, then that special flower has a more profound effect upon one's soul.

Maria, who was gifted and charismatic, was still attending college at Stony Brook University in New York. Moving to California would be a terrible inconvenience for her. Not only because of school but also because she was also extremely close to her family. I was also very close to my own family, and these factors were, of course, on that list of pros and cons.

What a difficult decision we had to make. Well, after days of thought, I came up with an idea. Maria and I finally agreed to take the leap and go out to California. I think we both knew that it would be a challenge, but sunny California did have its allure and appeal.

ME. This is Ken Rand. Can I speak to Dale Seymour?

JOLENE. Hold on a minute.

DALE. Ken, how are you. Thanks for calling back. Have you made a decision?

ME. I'm fine, how are you?

DALE. Doing great here in sunny California.

I was laughing. He's still selling.

ME. Dale, this is a very difficult decision for me, and I have come up with a compromise.

DALE. I'm listening.

ME. What if we do this on a trial basis, where I come out there for the entire summer and work for you, and at the end of the summer, we can both access if this is a good fit for both of us.

DALE. Ken, you may not believe this, but I was thinking about that same possibility. Let's do it. You can take a couple of days off at the end of the school year and then fly out and then get settled. We look forward to seeing you. You will love the people you are going to work with.

ME. Sounds great. I am also looking forward to it. I'll see you in a few weeks.

I had a strong feeling that the next time I would come to New York would be for a visit. By the end of the summer, both Maria and I decided that we wanted to stay in California. This cross-country move, however, did have an effect on our marriage. We were both on our own and very far away from family and had little if no support. Within a year, Maria and I were separated, and I firmly believed that the strain of moving to a new place with no family and friends was a key factor in our separation.

This all happened in 1977, and forty-three years later, after a three-year stint back in New York, I still live in California.

Dale, a former math teacher, and I hit it off right away. He was my mentor and I was his protégé. He invited me over to his house many times, sometimes for dinner or lunch or to just to chat. Dale had a beautiful home in the Los Altos Hills. The home was a one-story rustic-type home that was surrounded by beautiful trees and hills. There was no way he made enough money, as a teacher, to afford this home and property. I immediately knew that his company was doing quite well.

There were a few times when dinner at his home wasn't always pleasant for me. I was not a big fan of quiche or gazpacho, and I was too polite to tell his wife, Margo, that I was a meat and potato kind of guy. In fact, I had never heard of either of these foods until then. I don't even recall ever seeing quiche or gazpacho on a New York menu. I have had this problem about being asked to eat "unwanted" food my entire life. In the realm of life miseries, this is not at the top of my list, but it just seems to occur way too often to me.

As a teacher, I let my students know from day 1 that I am a big "chocolate" fan. My office at the community college had wall to wall chocolate gifts. Coming into my office was like walking into a chocolate museum. The main reason that all these chocolate gifts were still in my office was because they weren't my type of chocolate. They were nice to show off on display in my college office, but they were not eatable for me. Rude, huh?

This reminds me of another food story which I have saved for the next chapter.

Back to Dale.

Dale and I built up a great relationship, and we also played tennis at least twice a week. The first time we played, I'm thinking, *Should I lose? Should I win? He is my boss.* It didn't take too many Saturday afternoons to figure out that, one, he was very competitive, and, two, he was better than me.

After working directly with Dale on a few projects, he assigned me to work with a coauthor (Jan Fair) on some real-world math activity books. Within a few months, we published a series of books called *Handy Math: Focus on Sports, Focus on Travel, and Focus on Shopping.* Jan Fair is a gifted teacher from Santa Maria, California, and I believed she has also written a series of math textbooks.

After the project with Jan, Dale appointed me as director of research and development. Dale even gave me my own office. To me, this was a big deal. New York City teachers do not get an office. Not sure that teacher's anywhere get their own office (except in college?). I was beginning to feel important and a significant member of the company.

Part of my new job description was for me, on a weekly basis, to read and answer the hundreds of submissions from teachers that we received in the mail. These mailed submissions came to me on a daily basis from Idaho, New York, Hawaii, and from teachers all over the US (and the world). Teachers, writers, and inventors were asking our company to evaluate their possible future math products. It was a time-consuming job, but I loved it. I was about a year into this R & D position when I saw the Rubik's cube for the first time.

But first my story about "milk."

The answer is George Bernard Shaw.

Chapter Twenty-Five
(No) More Milk Please

Extra credit: Who said?

"Learning is not a spectator sport."

    a)   D. Blocker
    b)   Ellen O'Brien
    c)   Linda Sachs
    d)   Simon Legree

The answer is at the end of this chapter.

My tastes in food are very narrow. It's terrible. I know. As I said, I am a meat and potatoes and pizza kind of guy, and for some reason, I am always put into an awkward situation where I am invited over for dinner and the food being served is not to my liking. I know I am just supposed to be gracious and eat as if it the best meal I ever had, but it just doesn't feel right. Throughout my years of teaching, my students would constantly bring me ethnic foods to eat, and again I am in that awkward situation, especially when they ask me the next day, "How was it?"

The good news was that in the last five years because of extensive traveling, I learned to try to adapt to different foods. I am getting better.

Here is a story of such a situation that was the result of a trip to Europe. After my first year in teaching, my roommate (Jeff Winters) and I went to Europe for a four-week vacation. I could write a whole book about this adventure, but I want to get to the story about the "milk." A friend of Jeff's bought a Karmann Ghia, and we drove around Europe in this cute, little sports car. It was smaller than "little". I sat in the back seat the entire trip. Don't laugh, but there wasn't any back seat. There wasn't any room for a back seat. Where was a chiropractor when I needed one?

While in Europe, we visited the beautiful Mediterranean City of Nice. The beach in Nice was not sand. It was laced with stones, and if you didn't have sandals, it would be nearly impossible to walk on the beach, let alone get to the water.

Every day, Jeff and I would lay out a blanket, and quite often we would meet girls from different countries. I remember there was a group of girls, each one cuter than the next, who were all from Holland. I had a crush on one of them (Mira), but one of her friends had a crush on me, so, at least for then, it was not in the cards.

When I got back home to the states, I started to write to Mira (my crush), and to my pleasant surprise, she wrote back. She told me that she also had a crush on me. Each week for the next fifty weeks, we wrote to each other, and each letter became more and more romantic.

We both began to elevate a fantasy of being a couple. In May, of the next year, I received a letter from her inviting me to go to Holland during the summer and meet her friends and family. She also told me that she informed them that we were going to be engaged. I'm thinking the same thing. *This is crazy.*

What does this have to do with "milk"? Just be patient and wait.

That summer, I flew to Holland, and Mira and I met in Amsterdam and stayed there for a few days. I had no idea what to expect (wow, she was really cute). After having a great time in Amsterdam, Mira and I took a train to her hometown of Borne, which was a few hours away. The plan was to stay with her and her family for two weeks. Mira had a younger brother, Hans (of course), who spoke English, but neither of her parents spoke English, and this made for some interesting dinner conversations. Their home was an attached home in a lovely neighborhood. Kind of like what we would call townhouses.

It was at dinnertime when the milk story begins. Each night, her father would pour everyone a fresh glass of milk. And I mean very "fresh." It was right from the cow "fresh." It was one of the worst-tasting drinks I have ever had in my life. To make it even worse, it was warm. They did not have a refrigerator, not that one would have helped take away the terrible taste of the milk.

I don't know if you can imagine the dilemma I had knowing that I should be polite and not be the "ugly American." But there was no way out of it. I had to drink this god-awful milk. The worst part was that I knew, even before I sat down to eat, that this disgusting drink would be there, in front of me to drink every single night for the next two weeks.

With a false smile on my face, I forced myself to drink it. To help ease the agony, I would drink it real slow, only take a small sip at a time. This was absolute torture for me. This happened every night. Pretty soon, the two-week stay at her home was almost over, and I was looking forward to my last night of pain.

And I had a plan.

Here I am, on the last night of my visit, having dinner with this great family and my girlfriend, and a terribly tasting glass of milk. I decided that on this last night, in order to avoid the slow torture, I would drink down the entire glass as fast as humanly possible and get the pain over with. And that's exactly what I did. *Thank God that's over with.*

Mira's father noticed that I finished my milk. He looked at me with a smile of approval, quickly took the milk bottle, and filled my glass right back up again. The best laid plans of mice and men...Ha!

I spent the next week with Mira in her nearby apartment (thank God there was no milk), and then I went back home to the states. Mira and I were both too young to get romantically serious, especially in a long-distance relationship. Over time, our letters became less and less frequent until they finally stopped.

That was quite a digression. I probably should have saved that story for my autobiography.

The answer to the extra-credit question is D. Blocker.

Chapter Twenty-Six
The "Magic" Cube

Extra credit: Who said?

"The dream begins, most of the time, with a teacher who believes in you, who tugs and pushes and leads you on to the next plateau, sometimes poking you with a sharp stick called truth."

      a)   Dan Rather
      b)   John Brokaw
      c)   Barbara Walters
      d)   Lester Holt

The answer is at the end of this chapter.

In early 1979, as I did every day, I was sitting at my office desk at Creative Publications, opening my mail and reading through what people thought was the next great math gimmick. I say that because we rejected about 95 percent of all submissions. I soon became an expert at writing different types of formed rejection letters.

While reading the mail, I came across a bulky envelope from Hungary. *Hungary? Huh, that's weird.* When I opened it, out popped this colorful three-dimensional cube. The accompanying letter was from a US teacher who was visiting Hungary. He said that he had no idea about the origin of the cube but simply that it was known as the "Magic Cube." He said that the goal was to rearrange the colors so that each side of the cube was completed with only one color. He went on to say that he would do some more research about where it came from and added that he thought that our company would be the perfect company to mass produce it for the retail market.

Interesting. Very, very interesting.

I toyed with the cube and played with it for about thirty minutes and then frustratingly put it down on my desk. During the next few days, my coworkers would pass by my desk, look at the cube, and say, "What's that?" I told them, "I don't really know."

As each day went by, I found myself addicted to this stupid cube. I just couldn't put it down. It took me a few days, but I finally solved it, and that came with an incredible sense of accomplishment and dozens of submission letters left unread. I also immediately saw the marketability of this hands-on game. I knew that this would be the perfect product for our company.

Each week, the product development staff had a production meeting where I would present the best of the best submissions to everyone in the company. Of course, this "Magic Cube" was at the top of my list for our next meeting. My coworkers, however, were not that impressed.

"It's a gimmick."

"It's too difficult."

"It's too frustrating."

"It will never sell."

"Not something that our company should spend money on."

"It's not our market."

They were obviously wrong. There was this little voice in my head that repeatedly told me that Creative Publications could sell millions of these cubes, but there was nothing I could do.

In a few short months, there was a drastic change in the company. The vice president was able to convince the board of directors that they should hire him to be the new president of the company. This must have been a shock to Dale Seymour, who was not only the current president but also the creator of the company. This was not good for me. I was Dale's protégé. His leaving the company also made for a quick departure for me.

For the first time in my life, I am unemployed. *Ouch!* Not a great feeling. I'm not one to sit on my ass and cry, so I sent out résumés to a few other educational publishers and companies. One of them was the Cuisenaire Company, the makers of the very popular and widely used math manipulative called "Cuisenaire rods."

About a week later, I got a call from their president, and he invited me to go to New Rochelle, New York, for an interview. That was great news. New Rochelle was only about fifteen minutes from my hometown of Dobbs Ferry and going there would give me the opportunity to see my parents and the rest of my family.

I flew to New York, and the next day, I went to his office in New Rochelle. When I get there, we both realized that we have met before, and after greeting each other, he immediately asked me to sit down. Okay, get ready for this, the first thing I noticed was that the "Magic Cube" was obscurely placed on his desk. *Hmm?* I tried to pretend not to see it. *Coincidence?*

During the interview, I began to show the company president all the new games that I have been working on for the past two years. His face was lighting up as I spoke, and he (I wished I remembered his name) started to speak to me about some new plans for his company. He quickly got right to the point and said, "I want to start a new game division, and I want you to run it."

I'm thinking, *Okay, that's really very interesting.*

I am good at math and know that one plus one equals two. So, I'm now thinking that he wanted to manufacture and market the Magic Cube along with some of my games. I was also hearing, in my head, the Pointer Sisters singing their hit record, *"I'm so excited, and I just can't hide it."*

He told me that he needed a little more time to convince his investors that this new project was a good idea. He then asked me, "Are you interested?"

Well, let me think about it. I quickly told him, "Yes. It sounds like It's something that I would love to do."

We ended the meeting with things kind of up in the air, and he told me that he would get back to me after speaking to his investors.

All the while, he not even once ever looked at or even mentioned this colorful cube.

That night, I went back to my parent's home and waited for everyone in my family to come to the dinner table. Seated there was my mom, my dad, my brother Binnie, his wife, Linda, and my brother Frankie and his wife, Linda. I eyeballed everyone and turned to my dad and said, "Dad, do you have $50,000?"

His whole body was surprised at my question. "What do you need $50,000 for? Are you in trouble? What's her name?" He's always joking.

I then told my family everything I knew about Magic Cube, and I added on the possibility that I was probably the first one in the United States to even see it. I told my family, "There's no doubt in my mind that if we were willing to take the financial risk that we could manufacture and sell millions of them."

My dad and the rest of my family were not moved by my enthusiasm or excitement.

"It's just a gimmick."

"It's a big risk."

"Etc."

Well that was a dead-end. But wait, there's more.

While I was in New York, I went out to Long Island to visit a company called Great Games. A few months earlier, I just happened to be in a game store in San Jose, California, and I was there trying to show off my games to the store owner. One of the games I invented was a domino-like game that used half inch colored circles instead of small counting dots. I constructed my game into a handmade wooden box with very attractive domino-like wooden game pieces. (See below)

While I was at this store, someone walked over and asked me to show him how to play the game. The three of us, including the store owner, played the game, and the customer said that he was extremely impressed. He then introduced himself as one of the partners of a company called Great Games Inc. located in Long Island, New York. Another coincidence?

I knew I was going to New York to visit the Cuisenaire Rod company, so I arranged to go out to his company and show his partner my game. This meant that while I was in New York, I would be able to kill two birds with one stone.

The day after my meeting with the Cuisenaire Rod company, I took the trip to Long Island and met with the two partners (John and Bill) from Great Games. No, they did not have Rubik's cube on their desk, but they did like my game. And they liked it enough to immediately give me a contract for them to produce the game. They offered me a 15 percent royalty for each game sold. I drove back home to Westchester with a huge smile on my face. The next day, I had my dad's attorney look over the contract, and with his approval, I signed it. Yay!

A few days later, I received a call from the president of the Cuisenaire Rod company, and he had some bad news. He said that he was not able to get the copyrights to one of the games he wanted to manufacture (of course, it was the "Magic Cube").

I went back to California disheartened that I wasn't able to snatch Rubik's cube and make millions of dollars, but I was also excited that finally one of my games was going to be manufactured and put out into the mass market.

In a few short months, the owners of Great Games sent me out the completed product for my review. To say that I was disappointed was an understatement. The game that I showed them was made with an attractive wood with hand-carved insets for the colored dots. The completed product they sent me was in a small cardboard box with flimsy cardboard game pieces. You can imagine that I had some mixed emotions. I was happy that my game was on the market; however, I did not like the way it was manufactured. Oh well, at least the game was being marketed.

Below is a photo of their final product called "Dominique," and next to it on the right is the original game that I brought with me to Great Games.

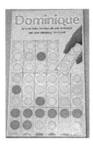

Oh. There's more to the Magic (Rubik's) Cube story.

About a month after my game, "Dominique," was released to the retail market, I received a call from the president of Great Games. He told me that they were able to get Macy's to sell my game in all their stores. The first store to receive it would be in San Mateo, California. He asked me if I would be willing to go there, stay a few hours, and demonstrate my game to customers. This store was only about twenty minutes from where I lived in Mountain View and made for an easy trip. Sounded good to me.

It was a Saturday afternoon, about a month before Christmas, and the Macy's department store was jam-packed with people. As soon as I walked in the store, I saw dozens of the Magic Cubes on display for sale, except they were now called "Rubik's cube," and this was in the men's department. As I walked through the store, I could see that every department in the store had Rubik's Cube on display.

I knew it. I knew it. Shit. Shit. I am pissed. I am not going to be rich.

I went down to the game and toy department, and they had a table set up for me with about fifty sets of my Dominique game. And right beside me, of course, was another display of about two hundred Rubik's cubes.

The good news was that I sold out of my fifty games in a three-hour demonstration. The general public loved it. I was also asked by customers to autograph a lot of those games. I'm a star? Not really.

The week after that, I was booked for another demonstration at the Macy's in Santa Clara. Of course, Rubik's cube was all over the place again. Again, I signed autographs and sold out my game. No, I'm not a star.

About twenty feet away from me was another table with another game being demonstrated. This game was called "In the Chips: Silicon Valley." There were boxes of this game stacked up to the ceiling. Sitting at that table was one of the inventors, Gary Suda. Gary and I started talking to each other and talked about the possibility of joining up together. I was impressed with him and his game. Below was a photo of me at the Macy's in San Mateo, California.

Meanwhile, Great Games, over a one-year period, was able to sell fifty thousand of my Dominique game. Not bad. That was great news. The bad news was that they had about four other games that they invented, and those games did not sell too well. It wasn't long before they had to close their company. *Now what?*

Within two months, I joined Gary Suda and his partner, Terry Bohme, and we formed a new game company called "Tega-Rand." Altogether, we produced and sold six different games. The toy and game market was a tough one. It was not easy to keep up with the Monopoly's and Scrabble's of the world. It wasn't long before Terry, Gary, and I ran out of funds and sponsors. *Now what?*

PS There have now been over four hundred million Rubik's cubes sold worldwide.

I had a major problem. I still did not have a full-time job.

The answer to the extra-credit questions is Dan Rather.

Chapter Twenty-Seven
My Calling

Extra credit: Who said?

"The art of teaching is the art of assisting discovery."

a)   Ken Jennings
b)   Mark Van Doren
c)   Ellen DeGeneres
d)   Jerry Lewis

The answer is at the end of this chapter.

I quickly began to look for some teaching jobs in the local newspaper, and I noticed that there was an available full-time teaching position at a local junior high school in San Jose. They were looking for someone to hire as an assistant principal of their middle school.

Well, here's my chance to be an administrator. I called the school and was able to earn an interview. I went through their entire interview process, all the way to the end. My last interview was with the school superintendent, which seemed to go even better than I expected. I even made a deal with him that if I was to be hired as the assistant principal, I could still teach one or two math classes.

When I arrived home, I immediately received a phone call from Al Plotkin, the assistant principal of my former school in New York City. The first words out of his mouth were, "Congratulations, Ken. Did they call you yet?"

I used Al as one of my references for this new position. Apparently, they called him for his opinion of me. Al was convinced that I landed the job. I spent the rest of the day waiting for a call from the school district, but it never came. The next day, I took the liberty to call them and spoke to the school principal. He told me that the position came down to two people, me and someone else. They choose the other person mainly because this person was currently a teacher in their school.

Ouch! That hurt. That was tough. Money was tight. *I was sooo close.*

Get over it, Ken.

I am now at one of the lowest points in my life. I am unemployed. I am separated from my wife, and things were looking hopeless. This was not a good place to be in even if you have high self-esteem, which, of course, was not me.

Shortly after that disappointment, I found myself fantasizing while I was walking from my car to my apartment in Mountain View, California. *I need a job. Quick!* As I'm walking, I noticed a sticker on the bumper of another car that said "Foothill Community College Faculty." Foothill was a community college in nearby Los Altos. I allowed myself to fantasize, *What would it be like to teach in a community college?*

I went to my apartment and made some phones calls to the dean of mathematics at Foothill, and as luck would have it (coincidence?), they needed someone to run their math lab learning center. I got the job. Yay! Foothill is an absolutely beautiful college with a sprawling campus situated right in the foothills of the Los Altos Mountains.

As head of the math lab, I supervised the record keeping for its students, and I was a part-time teaching tutor. About a few months into my new position in the math lab, I was asked by the dean of mathematics if I would substitute teach for a math teacher who was out ill. I, of course, said yes.

This turned out to be a turning point in my career. Fate? Coincidence?

The class was intermediate algebra, and it was jam-packed with over fifty students. This was my first time ever in a classroom with students in this age group. Most of the students in the room were probably in their young twenties. I prepared and brought with me some fun algebra worksheets, but I was still somewhat apprehensive about whether my games and activities would work, especially with this age level. The other factor, which was almost too obvious, was that students rarely cooperate with a substitute teacher, on any age level.

Another stroke of fate was that this just happened to be the day before "Martin Luther King" day. The first thing I did after introducing myself to the class was to ask them if it was okay for me to tell them a short story from my past. Students being students would rather hear stories than do classwork.

I went on to tell them the story of my former student, Michael, and the beautiful words he said to me the day after MLK was assassinated. The students were mesmerized. I had them in the palm of my hand. After I finished my story, I reviewed their current assignments, handed out some algebra worksheets, and did my best to interact and engage with the students.

That fifty-minute class session seemed like it was only ten minutes long. It went by so fast. I walked out of that room with a feeling that I had never had in a classroom before. Fifty students on the edge of their seat waiting for my next words or joke or story. I clearly remember after walking out of the classroom when I looked up at the sky and said, "Thank you, God." I felt like I had died and gone to teaching heaven.

Wow! What an incredible experience. I now knew what I wanted to do with the rest of my life.

The answer is Mark Van Doren.

Chapter Twenty-Eight
The Wheel of Fortune

Extra credit: Who said?

"Tell me and I forget. Teach me and I remember. Involve me and I learn."

- a) Benjamin Franklin
- b) Thomas Paine
- c) Thomas Jefferson
- d) Harriet Tubman

The answer is at the end of this chapter.

Wheel of Fortune

It was now March of 1979. I was still working at the Foothill math lab, but I should have been out looking for a full-time job. On this day, I was feeling lazy. *Wheel of Fortune* is one of my favorite TV game shows, and I tried to watch it on a daily basis. The show was usually on TV right before I had to go to the college and work in the math lab.

At the end of the show, I noticed a trailer on the bottom of the screen that said, "If you are interested in being a contestant, please send a postcard to the address on your TV screen."

Hmm? What do I have to lose? I am basically unemployed. I'm no longer attached. I might as well take a chance.

I sent out a postcard the next day and figured that I had only two chances to get picked to be on this show. Zero and none. To my surprise, two weeks later, I received a postcard from the *Wheel of Fortune* telling me that if I am really interested in being on the show to call the number on the bottom of the card. *It's becoming interesting.*

I called them the next day and proceeded to have a somewhat weird conversation with a member of their staff.

ME. Hi, I received a postcard telling me to call this number and let you know that I was still interested in being on your TV show.
STAFF. That's great. Have you ever been on any other game show before?
ME. No.
STAFF. "Well, there are some things you need to know so that you do not waste your time.

How can I waste my time? I am unemployed.

ME. I'm listening.
STAFF. Where do you live?
ME. I live in Mountain View, California. Why?
STAFF. Oh, it's just that we don't pay for you to fly here.

At that time, a round-trip flight to Los Angeles was $39. I was unemployed, but I wasn't broke.

ME. That's fine. I didn't expect you to pay.
STAFF. Well, that may be a problem because if you win, then you will probably have to fly out here again and then you may have to take off from work.
ME. Not a problem.

I'm unemployed.

STAFF. You also need to know that we interview about 2,500 people a week.

150

ME. Oh...that's a lot.

STAFF. I just don't want you to waste your time and money.

ME. That's very nice of you. It won't be a problem.

I'm unemployed. I have nothing to lose.

STAFF. You should also know that we only choose twelve people out those 2,500.

It definitely sounded like she was doing her best to discourage me. I know my odds were not good, but I had nothing to lose. I'm unemployed.

ME: Thanks, but I am willing to take my chances.

She told me that I would soon receive another postcard telling where and when to appear on the show. This was in early March of 1979, their postcard told me to appear there on April 20. On that date, I flew down to Los Angeles and took a cab from the airport to the Burbank studios. I should not have been surprised, but I was when I saw about five hundred people on a line outside the studio (do the math, five hundred people a day times five days equals?). Don't worry...no more math.

It was a beautiful southern California day. I arrived there around 9:00 AM. After waiting on the line for a few minutes, some of the staff from the TV show brought all of us into the studio and separated us into groups of fifty. We then received the royal tour of the studio and were escorted into ten different rooms, each the size of a large classroom.

As soon as we went to our seats, we found a questionnaire that needed to be completed by us. It was a pretty standard form, asking for our name, address, phone no., etc. It also asked us to list any of our accomplishments and/or hobbies. I did not write that I was unemployed but instead lied and said that I was a community college professor (a half lie). When I came to the section about my hobbies and my accomplishments, I wrote down that I had traveled extensively throughout Europe (which was true) and that I invented games that were sold in Sears, Macy's, J. C. Penney's, etc. (which was also true) and that I was a big fan of the *Wheel of Fortune* game show.

I was about to hand in the questionnaire, and I started to think, *Why would they choose me to be on the show? There are five hundred people here today. There is a good chance that only 2–3 of these five hundred will get picked to be on the show. Think fast.*

And that's exactly what I did. I pulled back my questionnaire, and without thinking, I wrote at the very bottom of the page, "By the way, I just happen to speak twenty languages fluently."

To this day, I do not know what possessed me to write this down. It was a total lie. I could have written that I speak five languages fluently or even seven or eight, but noooo, I chose the number twenty. The truth was that I have a hard time with English, especially with having a New York accent.

One of the members of their staff collected the questionnaires, and another staff member came into the room with a *Wheel of Fortune* test. Yes, a test. One thing was for sure, this game was so much easier when you were home watching it while you were sitting on your couch. On the test, there were about twenty fill-in the blank questions with some of the letters already there. The first four questions were easy. The next sixteen were impossible. *That's it. It's over. I am too stupid to be on the show. They will know this as soon as they correct my test.*

After the test was collected, another staff member came into the room, and she brought a TV monitor and a cameraman with her.

STAFF. How many of you really want to be on the show?
EVERYONE, *shouting*. I do, I do.
STAFF. I can't hear you.
EVERYONE, *shouting louder*. I DO. I DO!
STAFF. That's more like it. I brought a TV monitor with me because we want to see what each of you will look like on TV, that is, if you're lucky enough to get on the show. Any volunteers?

ME, *standing up right away.* I'm ready.
STAFF. What's your name?
ME. Ken Rand.
STAFF. Wow, you were quick to stand up.
ME. I want to be on the show.

I wasn't trying to be funny, but a few contestants laughed.

STAFF. Come on up here, closer to the camera.

My California assertiveness was paying off. Ha!
She then wrote an incomplete sentenced on a chalkboard and left some blank spaces and asked me to guess a correct missing letter. She said that if I made a mistake, then someone else in the room would be able to take my place. If not, then I could continue and go on and try to solve the puzzle. Meanwhile, the TV camera was rolling, and everyone in the room could see me on TV (except for me).

I could not believe my luck, I was able to complete the entire sentence, guessing one correct letter after the other. Not bad, huh? This was turning out to be a positive but somewhat long process. After I finished the game, another staff member came back into the room, and she had all our completed questionnaires. She told us that she wanted us to get up, one at a time, and talk about ourselves. She went on to say that the producers of the show were looking for people who had a TV-type personality.

I was now back in my seat, which happened to be in the last row, about one seat from the side wall. From where I was sitting, it became obvious that I would be one of the last people to speak.

One by one, each person stood up to speak. Meanwhile, I was sitting in the back of the room getting bored. There was absolutely nothing interesting about these other forty-nine people. At this point, I was beginning to feel a little more confident.

It was finally my turn to speak. I stood up and told everyone that I was a college professor (again, a half lie). I then went on to tell them that I traveled throughout Europe on a couple of occasions (a total truth). And then I told them that I invented some games that were sold in Macy's, etc. (also the truth). The second I mentioned that I invented some games, I could see the ears of everyone kind of perk up and their eyes open a little wider.

Someone sitting in the room shouted out, "What's the name of the games?"

I told them the names, and someone else said, "Can I still buy them?"

I said that I wasn't sure that the stores still had them but that they could try.

And someone else shouted out, "How much are they?"

I realized now that I was a hit. I was the "star" of the room. My confidence was growing. There were no more questions, and it was clear that I made quite an impression, so I sat down.

Just then the TV staff member in front of the room said, "Wait, just one second. You also wrote something on your form that is quite unbelievable."

I know exactly what she was referring to. *Oh, no!*

Someone in the group shouted, "What? What? What else does this guy do?"

Meanwhile I'm laughing in my seat because I know what's going to happen next. Still seated, I said, "I...really don't like to brag."

Now, all forty-nine other people were shouting, "What is it?"

Staff, "Do you want to tell them or should I?"

A very reluctant me said, "Hmmm...you tell them."

What did I get myself into?

"Okay, everyone, get ready for this," and she was now speaking very slowly. "He wrote down 'By the way, I happen to speak... twenty...languages...fluently.'"

There was a collective "Wow" from everyone in the room. *OMG! OMG!* I embarrassingly smiled, and all the while my heart was beating a hundred miles an hour.

Staff, "I think you need to stand up."

OMG, OMG. I really know what's coming.

She then said the words I knew she had to say, "I think this calls for a demonstration." She looked at everyone in the room and says, "What do you all think?"

What do I do now? Now my heart was literally beating outside my chest.

Everyone, "Yea. Yea. Let's hear it."

I was stuck.

ME, *in all seriousness*. Listen, it's a gift that I was born with, and I just don't like to show it off.

EVERYONE. Terrible excuse. We want to hear it.

ME, *now standing, with false confidence*. Okay, what would you like to hear?

Again, I had no choice. I was hoping that someone will shout out "Speak Spanish." If they do, then I could say "*Que pasa or Vente cinqo,*" which were the only two phrases that I know in Spanish. But to my misfortune, someone shouted out, "Speak Japanese."

ME, *thinking quickly*. Listen, I can speak Japanese if you want, but I have to remind you that I am fluent and that you won't understand a word I am saying.

Did I just say that?

EVERYONE. We're waiting.

"Okay, here it goes." And then I tried my best to look Japanese, and without any prior preparation, the following words came out of my mouth (using a very bad Japanese accent), "Mitsubishi, Toyota, sake, sayonara." And I sat down really quick.

The entire room broke out into a roar of laughter. The woman next to me was laughing so hard she peed in her pants. We kept this secret between ourselves.

Someone then shouted out, "Okay, wise guy. Speak German."

To which I stood up and clicked my heals and said, "Volkswagen, Dunka Schoen, Gesundheit." More laughter, and again I quickly sat down.

And that's how I got on the *Wheel of Fortune* show.

I appeared on the show on May 20, 1979, and went on to win three shows. I was lucky and hot. I won over thirty different prizes that appeared on a displayed showcase. At that time, they did not give away cash, only prizes. Of course, I had to pay taxes on the total value of those prizes. I remembered that I was very close to winning a car, but I had over $6,000 in my bank and did not want to risk losing it.

For the next thirty weeks, the UPS driver and I became the best of friends. He delivered a new prize to my door every week. It was like a year-round Christmas. The best prize I won was a trip for two to London and Scotland. I purposely asked after the show if I could delay this trip, and I did this for two reasons. I was still unemployed and did not want to pay all the taxes at one time. The other reason was that I did not have anyone special to go to Europe with. At least not yet.

As mentioned before, three short months earlier, I was in a state of depression. I lost my job at Creative Publications, I missed out, being ever so close, to becoming an assistant principal, and my wife (Maria) and I were having marriage difficulties that led to a separation and eventually a divorce. My old fears of not being good enough began to surface. My self-esteem was at the bottom of the barrel. Now, having been successful on the *Wheel of Fortune*, I felt like a "winner." My confidence in myself was now restored.

Little did I know that in a few short months, I would meet my wife to be. The beautiful, bright, and warm Vita (Isabelita Laurel). But I still didn't have a job.

The answer is Benjamin Franklin.

Chapter Twenty-Nine
Social Distancing 101

Who said?

"Students don't care how much you know, until they know how much you care."

    a)   Bill Gates
    b)   Tom Steyer
    c)   Mike Bloomberg
    d)   Anonymous

August 20, 1979

It was a night that is forever etched in my memory. It was four months after my incredible success on the TV show, and my confidence was sky-high. At this time in my life, I was now teaching as a part-time instructor at a variety of Bay Area community colleges. Though I had a series of part-time teaching assignments, I was doing this on a regular basis, and my income level was approaching acceptable.

My wife, Maria, and I had now been separated for about six months, and our relationship was continuing to go south. The depression and anxiety over the initial reaction to the separation was beginning to diminish, and I was allowing myself to build up enough confidence to try dating again. The truth was that, at this time, I didn't think I have ever been more confident in myself. Not sure what caused this, maybe it was because I was a winner on the *Wheel of Fortune* TV show or maybe I just got tired of feeling sorry for myself.

My friends and I were frequent visitors of the local clubs, and once again, dancing, which I know I am good at, was helping me build up that confidence. This self-assurance must have been obvious to others because I clearly remember, on a number of occasions, being in a nightclub, standing by myself having a diet coke (I wasn't a drinker), when out of the blue a girl would come up and ask me to dance.

This was quite a reversal of roles, and I clearly enjoyed it. This was a totally new experience for me. I never ever said "no" to anyone who asked me to dance. I was very aware of the pain of rejection that too often (way too often) happened to me when a girl said "no" when I asked her to dance. Little did I know that this would soon happen again to me, and it happened with the same girl, not once, but twice in one night.

It was a Wednesday evening, and I was at the local Mountain View club known as Bourbon Street. On this night, I was there by myself, just trying to unwind from the stress of driving to so many different colleges in one day. Bourbon Street was a very classy nightclub with an upstairs and a downstairs and a relatively large dance floor, although bumping into people while dancing was an occupational hazard.

While I was dancing with this girl, I noticed out of the corner of my eye a beautiful Asian girl walking up the steps to the upstairs part of the club. Beautiful does not quite do her justice. Her incredible eyes highlighted a confident smile, and her exotic black hair was long and down to her waist. *I had to meet her. I had to.*

I quickly told the girl that I was dancing with that I wasn't feeling well and excused myself. I then ran to the stairs hoping that I would be able to meet this strikingly beautiful image of a woman. It appeared that she was walking and talking with some girlfriends, but that didn't matter to me. I went right up to her and said, "Hi, would you like to dance?"

She looked at me and swiftly (too swiftly) said, "No. I just came here to be with my friends."

Again, under normal circumstances this rejection would have devastated me, but I was way too confident in myself to take it seriously. I was, of course, disappointed but was already planning to try again later. I continued to dance downstairs with other young ladies, hoping that eventually this exotic-looking beauty would come down and dance, but it never happened. After about forty minutes of waiting, I decided to go upstairs and give it another try. To my good fortune, she was sitting at a table all by herself. *Yes!*

So, once again, I approached her and said, "Hi again, would you like to dance now?"

She looked at me with eyes that were burning a hole in my heart and again said, "No, I'm kind of tired."

Oh my god, what do I do now?

Rejected again. I was beginning to wonder if I was too ugly or if I smelled or who knows what? How could she say "no" twice? Not knowing what to do or say and not wanting to give up, I said, "Well...do you talk?"

I mean, what could she say? *No! I don't dance and I don't talk either.* Ha! She then smiled and looked at me with those piercing eyes and said "Yes, I talk."

Now was my chance. Don't blow it, Ken.

I sat down and we began to talk. We talked about everything under the sun. She was so easy to talk to, and I felt an instant connection with her. Of course, I wanted to feel that connection, but I had never been more comfortable talking to a stranger in my entire life. I soon found out that her name was Vita (Isabelita Laurel), she was twenty-seven years old, and she was from the Philippines.

Meanwhile, as we were talking, the music was still playing and my body was moving to the beat, and the dance floor was filled with couples having a great time. Her table was right at the top of the steps looking directly down at the dance floor, and my eyes were fixated on her eyes and the dance floor at the same time.

After about thirty minutes of conversation, I looked at her with my best smile, and I said, "Would you like to dance now?"

Vita looked at me and sighed and somewhat reluctantly said, "Well, okay!"

It was almost as if she was doing me a favor or maybe she felt sorry for me. *Okay, Ken, do your thing.*

As we were walking down the stairs to the dance floor, the song that was playing changed from being a "fast"-dancing song to a slow ballad. My mind was now saying, *Yes, yes, Thank you, God.* I was actually going to be able to stand close to this beautiful human being and hold her near to me.

Not so fast.

I had danced with many young ladies and women in my lifetime, but I never, ever, experienced what was to happen next. Instead of dancing close like normal people do in a slow song, Vita put out her arms and basically held me off at about a two-foot distance. I was confused. I felt like I was dancing the minuet from the middle ages. I could not believe it. Now I'm wondering, *Maybe I do smell?* The physical space between us was so big that other couples could walk in between us. Vita was way ahead of her time when it came to social distancing.

I looked at her and laughed, and don't ask me why I said what I was about to say, but these were the words that came out of my mouth. "Vita, you know you can't get pregnant by dancing."

She broke out into hysterics as if this was the funniest thing she ever heard. Without another word, she slowly allowed herself to get closer and closer and closer. And, yes, she did get pregnant. But not by dancing.

At the end of the evening, I asked her for her phone number, which she gave to me. She then said, "Aren't you going to write it down?"

I told her that there was no way I would forget her number. She looked at me like she didn't believe me. I waited the obligatory three days, and then I called her. Forty years later, we are still very much in love and happily married.

What an incredible woman. Beautiful, bright, charming, funny, and warm. Even early on in our dating, we both found it to be remarkable how we were thinking thoughts simultaneously, almost as if there was a chemical connection. And her name is Vita, which means "life." She is my love, my wife, my life. It doesn't get any better than that.

We were also blessed with two incredible sons, Kevin, the eldest, graduated as a journalism major from San Jose State University and is now an editor for Apple in Austin, Texas, and Chris, who graduated UC Davis as a biology major and is a produce scientist for True Leaf in San Juan Bautista. And, ladies, they are both single. I am so incredibly lucky. Thank you, God.

Oh, I almost forgot. When I was on the *Wheel of Fortune* show, I won a trip for two to London and Scotland for two weeks. It was shortly after this show that I met Vita, and we planned to get married on May 31 in 1980, and this trip would be a perfect honeymoon. With about three months before the wedding, I called up the show to claim my trip. Here was my recollection of the conversation that followed.

ME. Hi, my name is Ken Rand, I won a trip for two to London and Scotland last year on your show.

THEM. Can you give us some more information like the date, etc.

ME. Sure, the show was taped on April 20th and shown on TV on May 20th of 1979.

THEM. Can you please hold one a minute.

ME. Sure.

About three minutes later.

THEM. Mr. Rand, we have some bad news for you.

ME. What's that? (I am already getting upset.)

THEM. Unfortunately, we no longer have that trip available. I'm sorry.

Wow, OMG?

ME. I don't understand. I was told by your producers that I could take that trip when I was ready. I don't mean to be rude, but I won a trip.

THEM. Hold on a minute.

How could this happen? I won a trip. They owe me a trip. About five minutes later.

THEM. Mr. Rand, we have a new vacation brochure for this year, and there is no trip for London and Scotland.

ME. Again, I don't mean to be rude, but I won a trip.

THEM. Well, I am going through the new travel guide, and it has a trip for two to Tahiti for two weeks, and it is equal in value to the trip to London and Scotland.

Are you kidding me? Wow. Tahiti? Exotic Tahiti?

ME. We'll take it. Can we leave on June 1st?

THEM. No problem.

Our honeymoon was on the beautiful islands of Tahiti, but we did not have a great time. I was sick almost every day from the local drinking water.

The answer is Anonymous.

Chapter Thirty

My Journey Continues

Extra credit: Who said?

"I'm not a teacher: only a fellow traveler of whom you asked the way. I pointed ahead—ahead of myself as well as you."

    a)   Arthur Miller
    b)   George Bernard Shaw
    c)   Mark Twain
    d)   Ernest Hemingway

The answer is at the end of this chapter.

For the next three years, I continued to be a part-time community college instructor. I was, however, still determined to fulfill my fantasy of eventually teaching full time in a California community college.

Each semester, I found myself teaching in at least three different schools, and there was even one year when I taught at six different colleges, and sometimes, I had to travel to three schools all in the same day. These colleges were not close to each other, and they were scattered around the entire San Francisco Bay Area.

Part-time (adjunct) instructors like myself were nicknamed "freeway instructors" because we literally had to drive all over the Bay Area to fulfill our teaching load. There were days, too many days, when I would eat breakfast, lunch, and dinner all while driving to the next school. Sometimes if I was lucky, one of the schools would offer me two classes to teach, and this would help to cut down on my driving.

If you're wondering why I wanted (or had) to teach at so many schools at the same time, it was because of economics. Part-time instructors were paid by the hour (class hour), and our pay was usually half of the hourly rate of a full-time instructor. The only way to make ends meet and put food on the table was to teach as much as physically possible.

Teaching like this for five years (1979–1983) began to take a physical and emotional toll on me. I was making good money, but I had to ask myself, "Was it worth it?" I desperately wanted to teach college full time, but very few, if any jobs, opened in my field of mathematics. No one wanted to retire and leave an open position. Why would they? Teaching in a community college was extremely rewarding and comfortable. Why leave?

One day, as I was looking through the *New York Times* want ads, I noticed a few teaching positions available in Westchester County, New York, which happened to be the county of my hometown, Dobbs Ferry.

I was now married and had a three-year old son, Kevin, who my parents have not yet seen. My parents were getting older, and now I was thinking about the possibility of moving back there so that they can share in our experience of his growing years.

I spoke to my wife, Vita, and as usual, she was very supportive and said, "Go for it." I was kind of used to her saying that. Vita has supported me in every big decision that we have had to make throughout our forty years together.

I applied for two teaching positions back east. One was at Mamaroneck High School and the other at White Plains High School. After having my interviews, I lucked out and was offered the position at White Plains High School. I say "lucked out" because at that time, White Plains High School was among the highest paid high school districts in the entire country.

This would be a big boost to my salary, and if I decided to stay, it would also be a secure position. The White Plains school district was in an affluent neighborhood and surrounded by beautiful homes and major companies, like IBM, AT&T, Proctor & Gamble, and Johnson & Johnson. These companies helped form a strong tax base which resulted in major funding for the school district.

This would be a new and different experience for me. It would be my first opportunity to teach on the high school level. Teaching on this level would now give me quite a resume of teaching levels to my credit.

First, I taught at the junior high school in the Bronx, then the community colleges in California, and now here at White Plains High School. I was, always, somewhat apprehensive over the task of teaching an age and grade level for which I have no practical experience. I was wondering how different could it be.

In terms of maturity, my high school students, whom I grew to love just like students on the other levels, were way more mature than junior school students, and they were not quite as motivated as my college students. But this was to be expected.

You already know that I am a big sports fanatic, so I made myself available to coach any sport that became available. Of all the sport programs that the school had to offer, I found myself coaching bowling and tennis. It was while coaching tennis that I noticed some personality differences in some of our students. To say that some of them felt "entitled" would be more than accurate. Some of the members of the tennis team was just not coachable. They thought they knew everything about tennis that there was to know. I remember many times, during practice, when I just did not feel comfortable with the apparent lack of respect from a few of the athletes.

It's not that I did not know what I was doing. I was a pretty good tennis player in the day. While living in Mountain View in California, I won both the class B men's singles and doubles championships. I knew I was qualified to coach even some of the best high school tennis players, but my comments and advice were useless to my players.

This sense of entitlement was not true of all my students, but it did appear that some of the athletes I coached felt a sense of privilege.

The answer is George Bernard Shaw.

Chapter Thirty-One
Brad

Extra credit: Who said?

"Education is not preparation for life. Education is life itself."

a) Arthur Miller
b) John Dewey
c) Patricia Cross
d) Ernest Hemingway

The answer is at the end of this chapter.

Talking about athletes. At White Plains High School, I had a male student in my intermediate algebra class (Brad), who was in his senior year. Brad was "all everything." He was the president of the student council, all-state in baseball and football, and he was never a behavior problem He was basically a nice kid. He had it all, except for the fact that he was failing his math class.

On each of his failing tests, I wrote "Please see me"; however, he never came after class to see me, not once. Not until one day, with about two weeks to go in the school year, when he finally came up to me after class and said, "Mr. Rand, I am just curious as to how I am doing in your class. I really need to pass this class because I have a number of possible scholarships waiting for me when I graduate in June."

I was in total shock that he asked the question, and you will soon find out why.

I looked right at him with a confused face and said, "Let's take a look at my grade book." I asked him to get a pencil and paper so he could write down his test grades as I announced them to him. "Okay, here we go. Your first test was a 45 percent, then next test a 37 percent, are you writing this down? Next test 52 percent and then a 40 percent and, oh, here you improved to a 58 percent, and on the last test you received a 47 percent."

He looked at me with a totally straight face and asked, "So, what's my grade?"

I almost fell right to the floor. After composing myself, I said, "Brad, it looks like a solid 'F' to me."

Then he said, "What about participation?"

Now I was beginning to doubt his sanity and mine as well. I told him "Brad, the only way you are going to pass this class is in summer school."

He then went on to plead his case on how I was destroying his future. I asked him why he never came to me for help especially when I wrote "See me after class" on every single one of his tests. His answer was that he was too busy with after-school sports.

He left my room a very unhappy man. The story was not over yet. That night, I received a phone call at home from his dad. I basically told the dad the same thing I told Brad and even read the test grades to him.

BRAD's DAD. I know, I know. He screwed up. But there must be something we can do to remedy this situation.

ME. Yes, there is.

BRAD's DAD. Great. What's that?

ME. He can go to summer school and take the course over again.

BRAD's DAD. That's not going to be possible. He is scheduled to visit over ten different colleges this summer. (*He continued.*) Let me rephrase my request. Is there something that I can do for you to remedy this problem?

Oh my. Oh my. This was a first. I was about to be offered a bribe.

"I'm sorry, Mr. ——. I don't think there is anything you can do."
I was beginning to get upset at his insistence.
His dad then said to me, "I am not sure if you know who I am."
Okay, I'll play along and listen to him.
"I am a very influential person in the community. I am the president of a major company, and I have enough money to help make life easier for you."
Now, I'm really upset. All right, that's it. I then told him, "Mr. ——, with all due respect, I am sorry, but your son is not going to pass his math class. There is nothing you can do, and there's no amount of money that can help him get a passing grade." And then I hung up.
Well, at least I have integrity. The potential bride wasn't tempting, not for one minute. I really don't know whatever happened to this student, but here is an example of the height of immaturity and a sense of entitlement. This was, of course, an isolated case, but I don't think things have changed so much in the last thirty years.
After three years of teaching at White Plains High School, I still had the yearning to teach on the community college level, especially in California. I was ecstatic that my parents were able to spend some time with us and our son. It was also great to be back in New York and have the opportunity to be with family and old friends. I am and always will be connected to New York.
I made some great friends at the high school. Among them were Pete Duffy, the math chairperson, and fellow colleagues, Sidney Crispell and Mark Benevento. Those Friday evening bowling tournaments followed by dinner are great memories.
Little did I know that my dream of teaching in a community college was about to come true.

The answer is John Dewey.

Chapter Thirty-Two
On the Road Again

Extra credit: Who said?

"I have come to believe that a great teacher is a great artist and that there are as few as there are any other great artists. It might even be the greatest of the arts since the medium is the human mind and spirit."

a) John Grisham
b) John Steinbeck
c) John Oliver Killens
d) Ernest Hemingway

The answer is at the end of this chapter.

In June of 1986, after teaching three years at White Plains High School, New York, I received a phone call from a former friend and colleague (Spencer Shaw) at San Jose City College in San Jose, California, where I had taught for one year as a temporary full-time replacement. He called to let me know that there were a few full-time teaching positions available in Bay Area community colleges and thought that I should give them a call.

One of those colleges was Hartnell College in Salinas, California. Even though I had lived in California for over six years, Salinas is a city that I had never heard of before. The other three teaching positions were all in Sacramento, the state capital, which was about a two-hour drive north from San Jose. The Sacramento community college system had three different locations in and around the city.

I applied for all the teaching positions, and because there were at least four possible opportunities to now teach at a community college, it was worth the risk of time and money for me to fly to California for the interviews. Once again, my wife, Vita, who also missed her family in Santa Clara, was in total support.

As soon as I arrived in San Jose, I drove up to Sacramento where I was scheduled to have three interviews at each in all three colleges on the same day. The Sacramento college interview committees and administrators did not want me to fly back for a possible second and third interview, so they decided that it would be easier for me, and them, if I had three interviews at their respective colleges all in the same day. Do the math. That means that I would have nine interviews in one day. My first interview would be with their math department, the second would be with the vice president of instruction, and the third would be with the president of the college.

This schedule had the potential to be very stressful and exhausting. It was 97 degrees in Sacramento on the day of these nine interviews, and I wisely brought a second suit. This was a smart move because after finishing the interviews at the first two Sacramento colleges, I sweat through my first suit.

After finishing all of those interviews, which seemed to go well, I drove back to San Jose to get a night's rest for my next day interview at Hartnell College in Salinas. Before driving down to Salinas, I did some research and found out that Salinas is an agricultural town and is known as the Salad Bowl of the world, and it was about a one-hour drive directly south of San Jose.

This rather strange and bizarre story of my interview at Hartnell College in Salinas, California (June 1986), seemed to me to be more of an attack on my credibility than an interview. It was just plain weird, and I had never experienced anything like it before or after.

I clearly remember one question from a veteran math instructor when he said, "It looks to me that you use a lot of 'gimmicks' in the classroom. Your students may be having fun, but how do you know that they are really learning?" His tone of voice and the way he said "gimmicks" made it obvious that this was not something that it saw as a positive trait for a math instructor.

I must admit that I was really taken back by this question. Again, it felt like more of an attack upon my credibility than a simple inquiry, and I was not prepared for it. This question was not a question that was among those on the list of questions that they had printed out for me. I thought for a minute, and my brain told me not to get defensive but just to try to prove it. And that's what I tried to do.

Included in my application packet, I had a statistical survey that was prepared by my former high school math chairperson, Pete Duffy, at White Plains High School in New York. This survey was conducted during the year before and showed how students from each math instructor did on their "universal" high school final math exams.

The average passing rate for the entire math department was 72 percent (over all math courses, grades 9–12), and my average passing rate for the same final exams and classes was 86 percent. It was all there, plain to see, prepared by my previous supervisor.

I pointed out this statistic to the instructor who had asked the question, and I passed a copy of it around for review to the rest of the committee, and then I said, "I appreciate your question, but I guess it looks like my gimmicks seem to be working." Though I felt offended by the tone of his question, I was trying not to sound smug or defensive or arrogant in my answer (which is not easy for me to do).

After this question, I was beginning to wonder where this apparent hostility was coming from. I instantly flashbacked to my earlier years in California when, because of my New York accent, some (not all) Californians had perceived notions about my personality. I clearly recall a couple of incidents when this became blatantly obvious.

In 1989, my brother and his wife came to visit us from New York. It was their first trip to California. I wanted to show them a great time, so I brought them to the beautiful city of San Francisco. We were near the famous tourist site of the San Francisco Wharf and frustratingly spent about an hour looking for an elusive parking spot. We decided it would be best just to wait by some cars, hoping that one of them would leave. Finally, after that long wait, a car pulled away from its spot. Just as we were about to pull into that vacated spot, a car, from the other side of the road, made an abrupt U-turn and took our spot. My brother was livid. He got out of our car and yelled at the other driver. The first words out of that driver's mouth was, "Why don't you go back to New York." *Wow!* It was difficult to try not to let this ruin our day.

One year later, I was in a supermarket in Mountain View, California, and I was on a long line at the cash register. I had only one item to pay for, so I politely asked people in front of me to allow me to skip ahead of the line. The first words out of their mouth were, "Why don't you go back to New York." Excusssse me. What did I do wrong? I did nothing wrong. I knew that it was my New York accent that caused their reaction.

These are just a few of many incidents when I felt an unjustified prejudice toward New Yorkers.

Back to the interview.

Then another instructor on the committee asked, "In your cover letter, you mention that there were other priorities that you have above and beyond having your students finishing and completing a course outline. Don't you think that your students will be underprepared for their next math class if you don't finish the course outline?"

Within a minute, two or three other instructors repeated that same question. Again, to me, it felt like I was on trial, and my crime was that I was not committed to completing the course outline. This was another question that was not on the original list of questions that they gave to me before the interview.

Math instructors are perhaps more concerned about completing course outlines than other disciplines and with good reason. Math courses are, for the most part, sequential, and therefore prior knowledge and preparedness for the next math class is extremely important. This question, I was ready for. I also knew that my philosophy of not completing the course was a little outside the box.

I told the committee, "My teaching philosophy is that I would rather wind up with 90 percent of my students remaining in my class and having them understand 80 percent of the required material than to have only half of the students left in the class at the end of the semester, understanding 100 percent of the material."

I then took the risk of saying, "I don't think it is my job to weed out or fail the weaker students, especially in the lower level math courses. I believe that it is my job to strengthen the skills of the weaker students and to challenge all my students to learn how to think." I went on, "I want to build up their confidence, not tear it down. If they don't pass the developmental classes that I love to teach, then their college future is over."

This teaching philosophy not only pertained to my college teaching, but it has been part of who I was as a teacher, regardless of which grade level I was teaching. Their body language and facial reactions to my answer did not make me feel very comfortable.

Again, somehow, I felt that some members of that committee had a preconception about New Yorkers. I soon found out that what some Californians perceived as confidence in themselves sounded like arrogance coming from a New Yorker. And what they felt were "assertive" actions appeared to be "rudeness" coming from someone from New York. I have now lived in California for over thirty years now, and all of a sudden, new friends and acquaintances tell me my accent is "cute and charming." Ha!

Well, I'm not sure how I made it through the first interview, but I was then asked to have a one-on-one with the dean of instruction and then another one-on-one interview with the college president.

Walking into the president's office, I was not feeling very comfortable nor confident. During the interview with the college president (Dr. Jim Hardt), it became immediately obvious that I had someone who was on my side. He seemed to be enamored with my background and was much more open to discussing my "teaching" experiences. Our interview (more like a conversation) lasted for over an hour, and our topics went from teaching to sports to life, etc.

In spite of what seemed, to me, like an overwhelming opposition from the hiring committee, and to my own amazement, I was offered the job at Hartnell. This position unfortunately was a

$24,000 cut in salary from my previous high school teaching job in White Plains, New York, which again just happened to be one of the highest salaried high schools in the country.

To make the decision even more difficult, White Plains High School had just offered their teachers a 10 percent raise that summer, making them, at that time, the highest salaried high school in the United States. To make my decision even more difficult, I was also selected for the teaching positions at all three of the community colleges in Sacramento. Even with the bad vibes I had from the interview at Hartnell, I chose to teach at Hartnell College and take the $24,000 loss in salary.

I chose Hartnell College for many reasons. Though my candidacy was accepted at all three Sacramento community colleges, taking any one of those positions would only result in only a $10,000 to $15,000 cut in salary. However, the extremely hot climate of Sacramento was one that I ever wanted to get used to. Life is strange. Guess where I now live? I live in Woodland, California, which is only 12 miles from Sacramento. And summertime in Woodland is brutal.

The day I drove down to my interview at Hartnell College in Salinas, it was a beautiful sunny day and a mild 72 degrees. Absolutely perfect! So, believe it or not, the climate had a lot to do with my decision. Another reason for my choice was that the Hartnell College campus had an atmosphere, a vibe, of "learning." Before my interview, I walked around the campus, and as I would pass by students, who did not even know who I was, they would smile and say "Hi."

I also saw a lot of students who were sitting on benches reading books and studying with each other. It is kind of hard to explain, but I simply felt like I belonged there. A third reason is that even though my wife and I were living in White Plains, New York, we still owned a home in San Jose, California, and it was within a relatively short driving distance to Salinas.

The answer is John Steinbeck.

Chapter Thirty-Three

There's More!

Extra credit: Who said?

"Teaching is the one profession that creates all other professions."

a) Confucius
b) Socrates
c) Unknown
d) Karl Marx

The answer is at the end of this chapter.

A few days before the start of classes at Hartnell in mid-August of 1986, the college had its traditional convocation day where the college president, Dr. Hardt, would speak to the entire faculty and staff about plans for the upcoming school year.

Before he got down to business, Dr. Hardt proceeded to introduce the nine newly hired full-time faculty. During his introductions of the new faculty, he spent about one minute on each of the new hires. In doing so, he spoke about their educational backgrounds and the teaching résumés of the new instructors, but that was until he got to me.

The president, for some unknown reason, proceeded to talk about me for about fifteen minutes, citing every accomplishment that I had ever had. He mentioned every single game I invented, every book I wrote, etc. I clearly remember sitting in the audience feeling extremely embarrassed as to the attention he was drawing to me. I almost wanted to hide.

After the convocation was over, quite a few faculty members came up to me and congratulated me and welcomed me to the college and said how impressed they were. The problem was that not one math instructor was among those who came up to me. My guess was that I was not their first choice for the full-time position (or perhaps it was my New York accent? Hmm?).

Without intent, the college president had put a target on my back, one that I had to live with for several years until I was able to "prove my worth" to the rest of the math faculty. It is my belief that one of the problems I was facing was that the math faculty, as good as they were and they were all very good, were traditional in their approach to teaching. Now that I was part of their group, these instructors had to work with someone who was totally nontraditional. Not an easy adjustment for both parties.

To my math colleagues, regardless of my nineteen years of previous teaching experiences, I was a rookie outsider. There was one math faculty member, however, who was a little more friendly than the others. His name is Chuck Beals, and he was kind enough in my first year at Hartnell to reach out to me and my wife and invited us to his home and also to a church dinner.

Get ready for a compelling story about one of my students, Dirk Etienne who was able to overcome an all too familiar learning obstacle only to turn it into an incredible experience of perseverance and success.

The answer is unknown.

Chapter Thirty-Four

Dirk Etienne

Extra credit: Who said?

"Every child deserves a champion."

    a)   Rita Pierson
    b)   Carl Sagan
    c)   Kim Tobey
    d)   Ana Banderas

The answer is at the end of this chapter.

Though my first few years at Hartnell were edgy, I was able to develop some great relationships with both teachers and students. About five months into the beginning of my second semester, while I was in my second-floor office, the first office I ever had as a teacher, I received a phone call from the president's administrative assistant. She asked me to come down to meet with the president, ASAP. I was somewhat anxious about this call because of all the previous trouble I had with Dr. Freyer in my New York City junior high school

When I walked into the president's office, there was a young man (about thirty years old?) sitting there in front of the president's desk This young man was very well-dressed, wearing a suit and tie. He looked like a movie star, and he looked like the suit he was wearing was rather expensive.

The president said, "Ken, I would like to introduce you to Dirk Etienne. You may know of his family. They own Tynan Lumber here in Salinas."

Ah ha! Dirk, who looked like a rock star, had a very expressive face and was obviously happy to meet me, yet he also appeared to be somewhat apprehensive.

Dr. Hardt told me that Dirk's dream was to go to a four-year university and get a degree; however, his fear of math has kept him from pursuing his dream. Dr. Hardt looked at Dirk and said, "If anyone can get you through your math requirements, it's Ken Rand."

Dirk looked at me with a hopeful smile. Dirk said, "Hi, Mr. Rand, I apologize for any inconvenience, but I need your help. This math is the only thing holding me back, and I have put off taking a math course for the past ten years."

DR. HARDT. Ken, are your classes full? How many students do you have in your beginning algebra class?
ME. I currently have forty-eight students in my class.

The limit was supposed to be thirty-nine.

DR. HARDT. Hmm? That's a lot.
ME. There are a few empty seats in the back of the room, and I'm sure I can find room for Dirk.

There were a couple of dynamics going on here. One was that I have had a difficult time saying "No" to students trying to get into my class. Another was how do I turn down a request from the college president? And yet another was how do I stop someone from pursuing their dream?

Dirk quickly enrolled in my class, and we made an instant connection. He was extremely grateful and appreciative that I made room for him in my class. He also kind of stood out in the class, being the only one wearing a suit and tie every day.

Dirk and I would often speak to each other after class, and I soon found out that we had a common interest in playing tennis. We not only had a good connection, but we also shortly became the best of friends. Dirk was very bright. He had no trouble receiving and earning an "A" in the algebra class.

The next semester, he enrolled in my intermediate algebra class and again earned an "A" average. I'm not sure where his fear of math came from, but it never manifested itself in my classes. Now, with the math classes that he needed under his belt, he soon graduated Hartnell, and he applied and was accepted to University of California Santa Cruz as a history major.

During the course of our friendship, I learned that Dirk was a talented musician and singer. *I knew it.* In fact, when he was in his twenties, he was the lead singer for a rock group called "The Virgins." His success with that group had him touring all over the world, and his face was on the cover of numerous teen magazines.

Dirk knew that my dad was a professional pianist, and he arranged for me and my dad to have dinner at his beautiful home in the Carmel Valley. After dinner, both my dad and Dirk entertained everyone with some great musical standards. Dirk was equally gifted at playing the guitar as he was a singer. What a night. Thanks, Dirk. Thanks, Dad.

Dirk was a rare individual who overcame his fear of mathematics to pursue his dream of graduating from a four-year university. And he was one hell of a friend.

A few years later, Dirk graduated with a degree from University of California Santa Cruz and invited me to his graduation ceremony. I was so proud of him. It's not easy having a dream that was blocked by a fear. He not only obviously had the ability, but he had that courage to overcome that fear and excel at the one thing he feared. This was very impressive. Thirty years later, Dirk and I are still friends. The physical distance between where we both live has been an obstacle, but I know that we are friends for life.

Coincidentally while reviewing this chapter, I just received a text message from Dirk that showed his new music video, "Hungry," on YouTube.

One of the things that I loved about teaching in the community college is that it fostered many of these great teacher/student relationships and friendships. It doesn't get much better than that. There are so many students and colleagues that I hope to thank for their trust and their friendship and plan to do so in the Acknowledgments of my book.

There is one other (actually there are quite a few) special students who, like Dirk, overcame their fears and anxieties of math in a way that is truly remarkable. Patricia Garcia and her incredible story is saved for later in the book.

In 2011, I would be involved in a fight for my own personal dignity and self-respect. It had to do with a textbook that I wrote and published.

But first, I would like to describe the Math Academy, which is, perhaps, my crowning achievement at the college.

The answer to the extra-credit question is Rita Pierson.

Chapter Thirty-Five

The Math Academy

Extra credit: Who said?

"The best teachers are the best story tellers."

- a) Jerry Lewis
- b) Dean Martin
- c) Frank Martin
- d) Ken Rand

The answer is at the end of this chapter.

In February of 2009, Stan Crane, our grant director, visited the math department meeting with some great news. The college was going to be the recipient of a $3 million STEM grant (Science, Technology, Engineering, Mathematics). Though the money was going to be split among several programs, he told us that this was our opportunity to make a difference in the lives of our students. He also told us that he was tired of grant funds going toward administrative goals and somehow never trickling down to the students.

I was easily inspired, and my brain immediately went to work. After the meeting, I spoke to Stan and volunteered to help. Stan had some of his own ideas and told me about a math program at Pasadena Community College that might be worth looking into.

Within the month, I flew to Pasadena and met with their program director where he described their Math Jam program. It was a summer program designed to prepare students for their fall math courses. He went on to tell me about the uniqueness of their teaching approach which was to use games and interactive activities to motivate and strengthen the skills of the students. Well, this was right up my alley.

I went back to Hartnell and told Stan that I would like to begin a similar program for our students. I didn't want to call it "Math Jam," so I called it the "Math Academy." I was soon named the director of the academy and quickly recruited two great teachers to help us begin our summer program with classes for two developmental courses.

We started with a total of forty-seven students, and word of mouth from the enrolled students soon propelled the program into an overnight success. Within five years, we grew to over two hundred students per academy, with preparation classes for math courses all the way up through calculus.

There were so many highlights from this program that I'm not quite sure where to begin. First of all, the program was free for students. They were also provided with free school supplies. Each student was also given a free T-shirt with the motto "EAT, SLEEP, MATH" printed on the front.

Perhaps the biggest perk was the free lunch. I made a great deal with the local Subway store and was able to get sandwiches at half price. Oh, we also provided the students, depending on their exit scores, an opportunity to skip their next math course. This was an attractive caveat for any student.

To me, the best attribute of the academy was the innovative teaching. About a month before each academy, I would hold a workshop for the teachers and tutors that I hired. I told them that traditional teaching (lecturing) was to be limited to forty-five minutes out of the seven-hour day. All other teaching was to be enhanced via games and interactive activities.

Though it was extremely rewarding for students to come up to me and personally thank me for this opportunity, my greatest satisfaction was when teacher after teacher would come up to me and say, "Thank you, Ken. After teaching in the academy, I will never teach the same way again." What they meant was that this innovative approach to teaching and learning would forever replace whatever methods they were using before.

I have some great memories from the academy.

On the next to the last day of each academy, I organized the "Amazin' Hartnell Race." This was a theme that I borrow and improvised from the hit TV show *Amazing Race*.

A lot of the academy students were new to the college, and I slowly began to realize that they did not know their way around the campus. Thinking about it, this was also true of our current students whose daily routine was "park my car, go to class, go back to my car."

In our race, each class would have about 7–10 teams of three students each, and they would receive a clue to help them go to a campus location. For example, "Find where the ghosts of Hemingway and Steinbeck like to hang out." The answer was "the library." Once they found the library, they would have a task to do. For the library location, they had to count the number of magazines on shelves directly in front of the library lobby. If they counted correctly, then they would receive a clue to the next destination, etc. There were over 150 magazines, thereby, making it difficult to count the correct number.

One of my favorite tasks for the students was to have their group count (individually) by sevens (seven, fourteen, etc.) until they reached seventy. Easy, huh? Not if you have a mouth full of potato chips. Winners from each of the classes would receive some great prizes donated by their instructors.

In 2012, the summer Olympics were in London. Boing! Why not have our own MathOlympics. Each group had to do five math challenges and five (very light) physical challenges (i.e., how far could they throw a handmade paper airplane).

It so happened that the college recently hired a new college president, Dr. Lewallen, and I invited him to see the academy in action. On the day of the MathOlympics, Dr. Lewallen came to visit, and he was there to observe over two hundred students having a great time of learning and having fun. I remember that he excused himself for a few minutes, walked away, and made a phone call. I was close enough to overhear him call a friend (another college president) with disbelief in his voice that college students were having so much fun late on a Friday afternoon. Good timing, huh?

One of the highlights of the MathOlympics was the opening ceremony I created. I asked the teachers to have their students march (like athletes) to the auditorium before the games would commence. Before they came into the auditorium, I turned off the lights. As they were walking in, I played the inspirational song from *Chariots of Fire*. It was an amazing scene because they were all dressed up in costumes waving banners displaying the name of their team (Mathathletics, Pi-Rates, etc.).

When they were seated, I showed them one of the famous scenes from that movie. After that, I took out a large candle and lit it as a symbol of the eternal flame of the Olympics. Then I said, "Let the games begin." The teachers had their students march out again onto the front yard, and we had a blast.

There were many great teachers in the Math Academy, but one teacher, in particular, really stood out, and his name was Johnny Perez. I believed I met Johnny in 2010. Johnny was twenty-nine years old at that time, and he was recommended to me by a math colleague as a possible teacher for the Math Academy.

After five minutes of interviewing him, I quickly saw a younger me. He had a passion and excitement for teaching that was contagious. I hired him instantly, and it was a great choice. Johnny quickly took advantage of this new teaching freedom in the academy and planned and executed endless hours of games and activities, which motivated his students to want to come to the academy every day. He had students playing games in the school hallways, in the courtyard, on the parking structure, you name it. Location was not an obstacle for Johnny. And he could teach. Wow, could he teach.

During the regular school semester, I had numerous opportunities as an evaluating mentor to observe him in the regular classroom.

His ability to "make it simple" and engage his students in their own learning process was a thing of beauty.

From 2013 to 2017, Johnny and I became a team. We were invited to a number of city, state, and national conferences to talk about the success of the Math Academy. We were still teaching at this time but took immense pleasure in presenting at these conferences where we could help other instructors learn how to engage and connect with their students.

Now that I have retired, Johnny has taken over the roll as director of the Math Academy. Johnny Perez (Dr. Math) could very well be the most creative, talented, and gifted teacher I have ever met. I know he is going to read this, so I need to remind him that he is the second-best teacher at Hartnell.

The answer is "Frank Martin."

Chapter Thirty-Six

Banned

Extra credit: Who said?

"If we teach today's students as we taught yesterday's, we rob them of tomorrow."

    a)   Ignacio "Nacho" Estrada
    b)   John Dewey
    c)   Benjamin Franklin
    d)   Ken Rand

The answer is at the end of this chapter.

In the latter part of my career, I would face my most challenging obstacle. The teachers in the academy were paid the rate of $65/hr. This was the going NIC (Not in Contract) rate for instructors who taught extra classes. After the winter 2011 academy was over, one of the school VPs called for a meeting between her, myself, and the grant director (Gary Hughes). Her first comment got us off to a bad start.

"Why are the academy teachers getting paid so much?"

Wow. This was not school funds. This was grant money that needed to be spent. Why did she care? And their pay was equitable with any extra instruction that teachers received when they taught above their regular teaching load.

Her tone of voice, and assumption, surprised me. I was shocked and upset. This went straight to the point of a supervisor trying to micromanage. To me, she just wanted to take control. Gary, the grant director, sat there with a confused expression on this face. I kind of felt that I was in this all on my own. Every time I needed something done or requested funds for the program, Gary found a way to make it happen. Gary was a huge fan of the Math Academy but not one to buck waves with an administrator. At least not in this meeting.

ME. I really don't understand your question.
SUPERVISOR. You know what I mean.
ME. No, I don't.
SUPERVISOR. I think we can make this work if we pay them $35/hr.

They can go dig ditches for $35/hour.

ME. I don't think so.
SUPERVISOR. Why's that?
ME. One, they are professionals and should be paid like professionals. And two, have you ever seen the academy in action?
SUPERVISOR. No. But that's irrelevant.
ME. I think that if you saw how hard these teachers are working and how much extra time they put in above and beyond the classroom and how creative they are in using a new approach to teaching math, I think you would offer them a raise.
SUPERVISOR. Gary, what do you think?
GARY. Well, I don't know.
SUPERVISOR. Give me one good reason that we can't offer them $35/hour.
ME. I can give you a lot of reasons, but the main one is that my teachers won't do it. They will quit. And so will I. And that will be the end of the Math Academy.
SUPERVISOR. Are you threatening me?

Take a deep breath, Ken. "No. I am just telling you the truth."

The meeting was now over. The next day, I spoke to the academy teachers, and they all thanked me for standing up for them, and each one echoed exactly what I told my supervisor, which was that they would rather quit than work for $35/hr.

By the way, don't ask me how, but the supervisor relented and allowed me to continue to pay my instructors at the current NIC rate. This rate, by the way, was the lowest NIC rate among the other nearby community colleges. The Math Academy was one of the most successful educational programs in the school. It gave our school prestige and notoriety. It was too valuable to the school in many aspects to disband it over a salary dispute.

This was not my last confrontation with this supervisor. In December of 2012, I received a phone call from a colleague and friend, John Sword. John and I had known each other for over twenty years and had both a good personal and professional relationship. John was trying to give me a heads-up about a student of his who recently failed his algebra class. John was a fan of my textbook *Beginning Algebra: Solving the Mystery* and was using it in his algebra classes. Apparently, this student had a difficult time accepting the reality that he had failed John's class, and he decided to blame it on my textbook.

John, of course, did not agree with the student nor his excuse, but this only made the student angry. Not receiving any condolences from John, the student then went directly to the college president and filed a complaint. He spoke with the president and told her about errors in my book and blaming those errors as the reason for algebra being difficult for him. The college president, being too busy for such a trivial matter, handed the problem over to her supervisor, the same supervisor that wanted to lower the salaries of the academy instructors.

What was once trivial became a crusade for this supervisor. This complaint became the perfect opportunity for her to "get even" over my resistance to her demand to lower the academy faculty salaries. She called me down to her office and on her desk was my book with page markers throughout the text. She went over every single page in the book to try to find as many errors as she could. Most of the errors, about 90 percent of them, were typos.

I need to give you some background information about how the book was published. In 1987, in my second year of teaching at Hartnell, I went to a math teachers convention and presented an idea for my algebra textbook to West Publishing. They instantly offered me a contract. Fantasies of making a lot of money from royalties were dancing though my head. *I'm going to be rich.*

College textbooks were very expensive for students, averaging about $150 to $250 per book. This meant that royalties on a published college text would be a great source of additional income. Most college textbooks have a long shelf life because of second editions, third editions, etc. This fact meant that royalties payments for a published textbook would last a long time. *I'm going to be rich.*

I should have done more research. I was very naive. It turned out that the West Publishing did not have a marketing department. They were what you would call a self-publisher for perspective textbook authors like me. Not only did they not have a marketing department, but they also did not have an editorial department. I even had to hire a private editor to work on my book. I also hired some very bright students to double-check the answers in the back of the book. So, instead of making money, I am spending money. *I'm not going to be rich.*

The book was completed in 1989, and I convinced the math department to allow me to have it sold for use it in my classrooms. This was no easy task. The good news was that the book had a very modest price of about $79. Unfortunately, after about two years, West Publishing told me that it was no longer worth their while to print the book, and in a letter to me, they gave me back the copyright.

My students loved my book. It was written for them. I wrote it so that they could read it without getting confused and frustrated. Now that I had the copyright back, I decided to go to a local printer and have them print it and split up my book into two volumes. I did this so that students would only have to lay out half the money in the beginning of the semester. This was important to me because I knew that students were paying hundreds of dollars on their other textbooks. Using a local printer also enabled me to lower the retail price to $29 for each volume. Not bad.

The printer asked me if I wanted a royalty adjustment to be added to the cost of the book. I said no. It didn't feel right for me to make money off of my students especially when they didn't have any choice but to buy my book for my class. So, for the record, I did not make one penny from the school bookstore from the sale of my book.

Back to supervisor's office.

She started the conversation by showing me the errors in the book and she said "This is unacceptable. I am going to advise the college president to remove your book from the school bookstore."

This was a lie; it was already removed from the shelves of the bookstore. "You're banning my book from the bookstore?"

"Yes."

I was at a loss for words. "You can't do that. I am protected by 'academic freedom.'"

"Good luck with that. I can and I will."

Wow!

Did she hate me that much? I couldn't believe it. She, or the college president, never thought of giving me the courtesy of asking me to fix the errors. I, and other math instructors, have been using my textbook in my classes for over twenty-five years without a single complaint. Now, there was one complaint and my book was banned. It didn't make sense.

I went to the faculty union president and filed a grievance. A week went by and did not even receive a response from my own union. I was livid. This was becoming personal to me. I then went and spoke directly to my union rep, and he told me that there was nothing he could do. *What?* I was too angry and frustrated to argue with him. My own union even refused to back me up.

I then went to the academic senate to plead my case. On a Tuesday afternoon, I went to their scheduled meeting, and unknown to me, about twenty of my students came and spoke, not only on my behalf, but on how the textbook made them a better student. During the meeting, I could see the outrage from some of my colleagues. It appeared that there was a lot of members of the senate who were willing to back me up.

At the next meeting of the senate, the supervisor came and did her best to destroy my credibility. Unfortunately, for some unknown reasons(?), some of the faculty on the senate actually took her side. After months of meetings, the academic senate eventually passed a unanimous resolution that condemned the actions of the administration, and it told the president of the college to reinstate my book into the bookstore.

Shortly after that, I had another meeting with the supervisor, and she offered me a compromise. She told me that if I fixed the errors in the book, it would then be available to my students in the bookstore. Though I offered that suggestion in my very first meeting, because it was her idea and directive, this suddenly became the obvious solution. This whole process took almost a year. Frustrating is too polite a word to explain my feelings. This was an unnecessary distraction of a teacher's valuable time.

Within a year, the supervisor and college president were looking for a new job.

As a said in my Introduction, my life as a teacher has had its share of ups and downs, failures and success, disappointments and highlights. To me, this incident was personal, but I fought, and I won.

On the opposite note, one of the absolute highlights of my career was the incredible "Against All Odds" story of Patricia Garcia as told in my next chapter.

This time the answer is John Dewey.

Chapter Thirty-Seven
Why We Teach

Extra credit: Who said?

"A good teacher is someone who can get their students to reach their potential. A 'great' teacher, however, is someone who gets their students to go 'beyond' their potential. To get to a place where the student, themselves, did not even think was possible."

        a)   Johnny Perez
        b)   Ken Rand
        c)   Kim Tobey
        d)   Frank McCourt

The answer is at the end of this chapter.

Patricia Garcia

This is an incredible story about a former student of mine, Patricia Garcia, who, in my third year at Hartnell (1989), was a student in my beginning algebra class. Her rise from the ashes of failure to the torch of success was an inspiration to anyone who knew her and to anyone with the hope of conquering their overbearing and paralyzing fear of mathematics.

Immediately after the first day of class, this young lady (Patricia was nineteen years old at that time) came up to me with a tear in her eye.

PATRICIA. Mr. Rand, I need your help. My name is Patricia Garcia, and I have failed algebra four times already with four different instructors, and I am about to quit.

ME. Take a deep breath and relax. Breath. Go on, I'm listening.

PATRICIA. You come highly recommended, and if I don't pass your class, then my dream of graduating college and becoming a child psychologist is over.

ME, *smiling confidently*. Relax. You have come to the right place. Together you and I will get you through this obstacle. I have total confidence in myself and an equal confidence in you. You made it this far. There's no doubt in my mind that we can do it together.

PATRICIA, *still a little apprehensive*. Is it okay that I come to you when I need help?

ME: My office door is always open. Relax. I will help you.

In all my years of teaching, I have never met a student work as hard as Patricia. She was relentless, and it paid off. Four months later, Patricia earned and received and "A" in the class. The next year, she took intermediate algebra with me and again received and earned an "A." This was beginning to sound all too familiar, isn't it?

This just went to show you how incredibly crimpling the fear of math can be. Patricia, like Dirk who had those same fears (in a previous chapter), graduated Hartnell and, also like Dirk, went on to attend and graduate from University of California Santa Cruz. Because of Patricia's remarkable success story, which you are soon to read about, I felt compelled to offer her my recommendation for the 2014 Distinguished Alumna Award which would be presented at the year's end graduation ceremony.

A few weeks later, Patricia received the following letter from the president of the college.

Dear Ms. Garcia,

Congratulations! You have been selected as the 2014 Hartnell College Distinguished Alumna and Commencement Speaker. This honor is conveyed to former students of Hartnell College who have made significant achievements in their field or in service to our community. The governing board was particularly impressed with your professional accomplishments, your commitment to community service, and your exceptional leadership in many areas. You clearly serve as a valuable mentor for our students.

Commencement will take place on Friday, May 30, 2014, 6:30 PM in the Hartnell College Gymnasium. On this same day, a reception will be held to recognize our distinguished guests. The governing board and others will gather in building B, room 208 at 5:00 PM. At around 6:15 PM, you will be a member of the procession into the gymnasium with the trustees and other college officials.

We are pleased that you will be able to join us at this very special time and help our students appreciate the honored company they will now keep as alumni of this college.

Congratulations again.

Sincerely,
William Lewallen, PhD
Superintendent/President

Patricia called me the next day and thanked me for the nomination. I called her a few days before the graduation ceremony and asked her if she wanted me to review her speech. She said, "Thank you, but I rather you wait until the ceremony so you can hear it for the first time."

With her permission, below is a copy of her speech.

Dear Graduating Class of 2014,

I am honored and humbled as I stand before you today in celebration of your hard work and accomplishments. The flood of memories of my own struggles that I had to face and endure, in order to once sit where you are today, are so vibrant to me at this very moment.

When I came to Hartnell College, I was really excited about my classes, but I was nervous about stepping forward. What made me even more nervous was that I had failed algebra twice in high school, and because of that, I lost the opportunity to attend UC Santa Cruz.

From there on, I had a fear of failing algebra and had severe math anxiety. At Hartnell College, I continued to fail algebra two more times! Now count with me, twice in high school and two more times at Hartnell. Yes, that makes four times!

At this point, I needed to look for a teacher that best fit my learning style; at that time, I did not realize that I had attention deficit disorder and dyslexia. I know! What a combination!

What I did have was a self-fulfilling prophecy that I would continue to fail, but with Mr. Rand, everything somehow changed, and he found a way to have math make sense and most importantly fun. Education can work! Don't ever give up on dreaming. You can do anything you set your heart or mind to, lift yourself up, and work hard.

I took my two required math classes with Mr. Rand and was able to receive an "A" in both of them. This is unbelievable considering I had failed algebra four times before. I was then able to transfer to UC Santa Cruz where I studied psychology. My goal at the time was to become a child psychologist.

After graduating from UC Santa Cruz with my bachelor's degree, I took a year off to save for graduate school. Needing to pay the bills, I then became a substitute teacher in the Salinas school district, and after just two weeks into it, I was asked to teach middle school math for thirty days I thought to myself, How hard could it be to teach seventh-grade math? I admit, I was apprehensive at that thought, having my own math experiences.

After thirty days of teaching, I became inspired. I could not continue in that position without enrolling in a teacher credential program. I fell in love with my students, and I fell in love with teaching. I now decided to change my career! I truly believe everything happens for a reason.

At one time, I feared math! Okay, let's be honest, I avoided it! Now I loved teaching math! How did this happen? I know! It was because of teachers like Mr. Rand! He changed my life in so many ways. He believed in me and supported me. He would not let me fail. He was tough when he needed to be and gentle at the precise moments when I felt like quitting. Mr. Rand, can you please stand? I would like to take this opportunity to thank you for changing my life and the lives of thousands of students you have touched.

When I graduated here at Hartnell College over twenty-two years ago, I was so certain that

I wanted to be a child psychologist. As it turned out, I had many occupations. A teacher is a counselor, a nurse, a detective, a mentor, a coach, a surrogate parent, and, yes, even a child psychologist. I have spent twenty amazing years teaching because I did not run away from fear. Ed Helms said it best, "Don't be afraid of fear. Because it sharpens you, it challenges you, it makes you stronger, and when you run away from fear, you also run away from the opportunity to be your best possible self."

Today, graduates, it is about you being your best possible self. You have pursued and accomplished an education that will open many doors for you. Education brings us knowledge, it leads us to careers, it builds our character, it leads to enlightenment, and it helps our world to progress.

Nelson Mandela, who was an inspiration to us all, said, "Education is the most powerful weapon which you can use to change the world." So, graduates, I ask you today, "How will you use your education to change the world? How will you give back to your communities?" Today you are different from the first day you walked through the doors of Hartnell College. It has been said, "With power comes great responsibility," but I say, "With an education comes great power and responsibility."

Graduates, failing algebra was only one of many obstacles that I had to overcome, and life brought me many more. Within these life experiences, I have stumbled and even fallen down, but I want you to remember this, there is no such thing as failure, and I am living proof.

I am in agreement with Oprah on failure. "Failure is just life trying to move us in another direction. The key is to learn from every mistake because every experience, particularly your mistakes, are there to teach you. In life, we will fail, but it is important to remember that failure does not define us. Maybe things did not go as you hoped, but shake off your disappointment and create a new vision for yourself."

So, graduates, who will you aspire to be? How will you rise to the occasion? What footprint will you leave on our planet? Whose life will you change?

I like to leave you with a poem that has inspired me. This famous inspirational poem challenges us to accept responsibility for our lives no matter our circumstances.

We are the master of our destiny. We are responsible for our own happiness. Invictus in Latin means unconquered. My hopes for you are to live your lives in such a way, unconquered!

Invictus
William Ernest Henley

Out of the night that covers me,
Black as the Pit from pole to pole,
I thank whatever gods may be
For my unconquerable soul.

In the fell clutch of circumstance
I have not winced nor cried aloud.
Under the bludgeonings of chance
My head is bloody, but unbowed.

Beyond this place of wrath and tears
Looms but the Horror of the shade,
And yet the menace of the years
Finds, and shall find, me unafraid.

It matters not how strait the gate,
How charged with punishments the scroll,
I am the master of my fate:
I am the captain of my soul.

Though I was grateful and proud of Patricia's unexpected praises, her story was not about me. I have nothing but overwhelming pride in her accomplishments considering the obstacles she had to overcome. What she didn't tell you was that she went on to become the department chair and instructional lead at her school. There's more. Not satisfied with that position, she went on to become an assistant principal. And she was not finished yet. Patricia is now taking her Doctorate in Learning and Instruction.

From 2009 through 2015, Patricia took on the added responsibility of working for me in my summer and winter Math Academies at Hartnell College. To this day, Patricia and I are still friends.

Both Dirk and Patricia have extraordinary stories. They both were exceptional students, but they were not the exception. It was difficult to express the respect I have for all my students who on a daily basis were faced with obstacles that would deter most of us from even trying.

So to answer the question of why we teach, I'll start by stating the wrong reasons. We do not teach for the money. We do not teach for the praises nor the awards that come along with excellence. We teach for the almost euphoric feeling of having been able to make a difference in the lives of our students, even if it's just "one student at a time."

Now you know why we teach.

The answer to the extra-credit question is me (Ken Rand). This was a response I gave to a college journalist who asked about the difference between a good teacher and a great teacher. It was not an answer that I had to think about.

Chapter Thirty-Eight
It's Time to Hang Them Up

Extra credit: Who said?

"Every ending is a new beginning."

a) Johnny Perez
b) Marianne Williamson
c) Kim Tobey
d) Frank McCourt

How do you know when it's the right time to retire?

If you took a survey of those who have retired, I believe the most common answer is "You just wake up one morning and you know that it's time."

Well, that was exactly what happened to me. In early July, about a month after Patricia's speech to the 2014 graduating class at Hartnell, I woke up, and this feeling came over me that said, "It's time." I thought I could and should teach one more semester and then retire that January. I didn't retire immediately because I had too many students in the previous semester that were looking forward to taking their next math class with me, and I did not just want to leave them hanging.

The time was right for many reasons. Both my body and mind told me that I needed a rest. Forty-seven years of teaching without a break is a long time. Unfortunately, my college did not offer any sabbaticals, otherwise I would probably still be teaching.

I remember many years ago when I was interviewed by the college journalist who was writing an article about me. During the interview, he asked, "Where do you get your motivation from to inspire your students?"

My first response was "My motivation comes from my fear of failure." I went on to tell him about how poorly my algebra students did in my first year of teaching. "This was a heartbreaking moment for me, and I never wanted to experience it again." Then I continued, "By the way, you have it backwards." He gave me a quizzical look. "It is not me who inspires my students, it is my students who inspire me."

He asked, "How so?"

"If, as instructors, we allow ourselves to listen and learn from our students especially about the incredible obstacles they face and overcome on a daily basis, it is easy for me to get inspire. They come to our classes with a dream of graduating college and creating a better life for themselves and their family. Who am I to get in the way of that dream? My job is to foster that dream and make it a reality."

I believe that the most important changes in education over the last twenty years are how today's teachers have learned to adapt to the vast variety of different learning styles of students. When I first began my teaching career, "connecting and engaging" with students was an unknown resource. Today's teachers, especially my Hartnell colleagues, have made this resource a daily reality. Our students are in good hands.

I have spent the last twenty-eight years of my teaching career at Hartnell College. Over the span of forty-seven years, I have teaching experiences that cover many different schools on a variety of levels. I can honestly say, without reservation, that the teaching faculty at Hartnell is the best that I have ever worked with.

Early on in my teaching career, even as soon as within a few months into my first teaching position, I became overwhelmed with the wide array of problems that my students brought with them to school. In each class, there were students who were absent, students who were late, then, of course, there were those who did not do their homework and add to this the inevitable one or two discipline problems. Multiply this by five classes and before I knew it, I had as many as thirty students who were in dire need of extra supervision and perhaps some TLC.

What to do? What to do?

It was then when I decided upon my approach to alleviate some of these problems. First, I would talk to the student and let them know I am concerned. "Are you late because someone is driving you to school? Let's see if we can work on that." Or "When I was in school, I didn't do my homework because I was lazy. Do you have a similar problem, or is the homework too difficult?"

If my "one-on-one" with them did not have any effect and if the conduct continued, then I would call their home. The first time I would call, I would speak to the student, but the student knew that it was only a matter of time that I would want to talk to their parent.

Unfortunately, I can see that in today's climate of political correctness, it would be difficult to imagine using this technique. Especially with a student of the opposite sex. This is sad because at that time in my career, calling home became an extremely effective tool for me.

Perhaps now you will understand why I choose the title for my book. The one thing that stood out for me among the vast number of students who needed my "individual" help is that I needed to try to remove these obstacles "one student at a time." Looking back, I think it worked.

Yes, I do miss teaching, especially the great relationships I had with my colleagues and students, but I am enjoying my retirement. My dream job now would be to teach education courses at a four-year college, but it's not easy getting this type of teaching position. Maybe this book will help? However, there is good news. I still have more work to do and more stories to tell.

To my former students, sometimes I have difficulty expressing my feelings in words. So I think I have the perfect song to show how I feel about all of you. You are welcomed to get out of your chairs and dance. The song is from the movie *Dirty Dancing*.

Now, I've had the time of my life
No, I've never felt this way before
Yes, I swear it's the truth
And I owe it all to you...

The answer is Marianne Williamson.

About the Author

Ken Rand is an award-winning college math professor who retired in 2015 after forty-seven years of teaching. Soon after retirement, Ken became a presenter and guest speaker at numerous statewide and national educational conferences. The encouraging feedback he received from those who have attended those presentations is one of the reasons that he decided to write his book.

Ken's teaching experiences include a variety of educational levels beginning with junior high school, high school, and then two- and four-year colleges. For a brief period, he was also the director of research and development for Creative Publications, a mathematics educational publisher.

While working for Creative Publications, Ken wrote and edited a variety of activity books and created some classroom games. He has also written an algebra textbook (published by West Publishers) called *Solving the Mystery*. Some of the strategy games that he created have been sold in retail stores such as Macy's and J.C. Penney, and stores throughout Canada and Europe.

More recently, he was one of the coauthors and contributors of the book *Habits of the Mind* (Stylus Publishers) and has self-published his own book of word games titled *Afterwords*.

Ken's crowning achievement at Hartnell College just may be his creation and development of the Math Academy, an extremely successful summer and winter program designed to prepare students for their next math course. This unique and successful program became a model for similar programs throughout the country.

Known for his classroom story-telling technique, Ken has found a way to bring those classic classroom experiences to life in his book *One Student at a Time*.

After reading Ken's book, you will begin to realize that Ken has dedicated his professional life to making a difference in the lives of his students. Not only has Ken inspired his students, but perhaps Ken's greatest impact is on the many teachers who have been fortunate enough to attend his interactive workshops. Those who have participated left with comments such as, "I will never teach the same way again," and "When are you available to perform a workshop at my school?"

In 1967, when Ken first became a teacher, he was a pioneer in introducing innovative and interactive classroom activities that helped him to connect and engage with his students. The words "Master Teacher" are rarely used to described today's great teachers, but this is exactly what some of his supervisors have written about him in their classroom evaluations.

CPSIA information can be obtained
at www.ICGtesting.com
Printed in the USA
LVHW072036111021
700151LV00020B/2389